Beyond the Cross and the Sword

The Rise and Fall of the Templars

by Claudio Bocchia - Sigma Thotmes publishing - all rights reserved.

It is illegal to reproduce, duplicate or transmit any part of this document, whether electronically or in print. Recording this composition is strictly prohibited.

Dear Reader,

Welcome to *Templars: Beyond the Cross and the Sword*. I am Claudio Bocchia, a writer with a passion for historical mysteries. This book explores the fascinating history of the Templars, a military and religious order that profoundly influenced medieval Europe.

In it, I examine their organization, daily life, and the strict rules that governed them, as well as the epic battles, wealth they accumulated, and the political intrigues that marked their history.

Beyond simply recounting the facts, the book analyzes the impact of the Templars on medieval society and delves into the legends surrounding them, revealing how their legacy has transformed over the centuries.

This work is for anyone fascinated by medieval history and the mysteries of that era, offering a captivating exploration of an order that continues to influence our imagination.

Your feedback is valuable to me, and I would love to hear your thoughts. Reader reviews are essential for helping others discover this book. If you enjoyed reading it, please consider sharing your experience. It would bring me great joy and be immensely helpful.

I hope you enjoy reading this book as much as I enjoyed writing it. Thank you, and happy reading!

Claudio Bocchia

Foreword 7

Introduction. 8

Chapter 1: The Foundation of the Order. 11

    Historical context of the Crusades. 11

    The Beginnings of the Order (1118). 13

    Devotion and Admiration. 14

    The Support of Saint Bernard of Clairvaux. 15

    The Official Recognition by the Pope. 18

    Mission and objectives of the Templars. 20

Chapter 2: The Rise of the Templars. 23

    The Rule of the Templars. 23

    The Rapid Expansion and Establishment of Commanderies. 26

Chapter 3: The Organization and Life within the Order. 30

    Hierarchical Structure of the Templars. 30

    Daily Life of the Knights Templar. 33

    Rituals and Religious Practices of the Knights Templar. 37

Chapter 4: The Military Campaigns. 41

    Participation in the Crusades: The Key Role of the Templars in the Crusades. ...41

    At the Heart of the Battle: The Greatest Battles and Sieges of the Templars. ...57

    Strategic Role of the Templar Fortresses. 72

Chapter 5: The Economy and Possessions of the Templars. 76

    The Commanderies and Land Properties of the Templars. 76

    Banking and Economic Activities of the Templars. 80

    Economic Influence of the Templars in Europe and the East. 83

Chapter 6: The Decline and Fall of the Order. 88

Conflicts with European Sovereigns. 88

The Arrest Warrant and the Day of Friday, October 13, 1307. 91

The Accusations and Torture of the Templars. 95

The Trials of the Templars in France. 98

The Trials of the Templars in Other Countries. 101

The Dissolution of the Order by the Pope. 104

The Flight of the Templars to Portugal and Scotland. 107

The Suspicions of Templar Presence in America. 110

The Treasure of the Templars: The Different Theories. 113

The Likely Hideouts. 114

The Templar Artifacts discovered by Hamilton White and Carl Cookson. 116

Chapter 7: The Legacy of the Templars. 119

Influence on Subsequent Military Orders. 119

Legends and Myths around the Templars. 122

Chapter 8: Timeline of Major Events. 126

Foundation and Ascension (1118-1147). 126

Expansion and Power (1147-1291). 126

Decline and Betrayal (1307-1314). 127

Heritage and Legends (1314-present). 127

Two Centuries of Holy Wars. 128

Pivotal Dates in the History of the Templars. 128

Chapter 9: Chronology of the Grand Masters of the Templars. 130

I. Hugues de Payens (de Paganis) 1118 — 1136. 130

II. Robert de Craon, known as the Burgundian (1136-1147). 132

III. Evrard des Barres (1147-1149). 134

IV. Bernard de Tremelay (1149-1153). 136

V. Bertrand de Blanquefort (1153-1168). 138

VI. Philip of Nablus (1168-1174). *140*

VII. Odon de Saint-Amand (1171-1179). *141*

VIII. Alan or Arnaud de Toroge (1179-1184). *143*

IX. Terric (Terricus) (1184-1188). *144*

X. Gerard de Ridefort (1188-1189). *146*

XI. Robert de Sablé (1191-1196). *147*

XII. Gilbert Horal or Hérail (1196-1200). *148*

XIII. Philippe de Plessiez (1201-1217). *150*

XIV. William of Chartres (1217-1219). *151*

XV. Pierre de Montaigu (1219-1233). *152*

XVI. Armand de Périgord (1233-1234). *153*

XVII. Guillaume de Sonnac (1247-1250). *154*

XVIII. Renaud de Vichiers (1250-1256). *156*

XIX. Thomas Béraut or Bérail (1256-1273). *157*

XX. Guillaume de Beaujeu (1273-1294). *158*

XXI. Thiébaud Gaudin or Monk Gaudini (1291-1298). *160*

XXII. Jacques de Molay (1298-1314). *162*

Chapter 10: Connections Between the Templars and Pirates. **165**

The Fall of the Templars and the Flight to the Sea. *165*

Chapter 11: Templars and Freemasons: Historical Links. **168**

The Origins of the Templars and Freemasons. *168*

Chapter 12: Lessons Learned from the History of the Templars. **172**

Foreword.

Dear reader,

The shadow of mystery still envelops the history of the Templars, a military and religious order whose greatness and fall continue to captivate and challenge our understanding. These knights, dedicated to the defence of faith and pilgrims, have left behind legends and enigmas that persist through the ages, reminding us that reality can often surpass fiction. This book is a dive into the depths of the most fascinating and mysterious stories of the Templars, where the answers seem as elusive as the stars in a night sky.

The history of the Templars confronts us with fundamental questions about faith, power, and justice. What does the persecution and dissolution of this order reveal about medieval power dynamics? What lessons can we draw from the accusations made against them and the trials that followed? How have the Templars continued to influence our culture and collective imagination, from the Crusades to the present day?

This work is an invitation to look beyond established historical facts, to question traditional narratives and to deeply reflect on the implications of the quest for truth and justice in a complex and often ruthless world. With an open and critical mind, join us in this exploration of Templar enigmas, from sacred relics to secret manuscripts, from buried treasures to mysterious rituals. Perhaps together, we will get closer to the answers that so many researchers, historians and enthusiasts have desperately sought.

Introduction.

The shadow of the Templars still looms over history, surrounded by mysteries and legends. The Crusades were the scene of major upheavals, but it is the enigmas and secrets of the Templars that continue to captivate the imagination. This book explores the origins and exploits of these knights, from their birth in the turmoil of the Crusades to their mysterious disappearance.

The Holy Land, a region laden with spiritual and historical significance, is the cradle of the three major monotheistic religions: Judaism, Christianity, and Islam. Located in the heart of the Middle East, it encompasses holy places such as Jerusalem, Bethlehem, and Nazareth. For Christians, it represents the stage for the key events in the life of Jesus Christ, from his birth to his crucifixion and resurrection. It is this sacred land, imbued with mysticism and conflicts, that the Templars had sworn to protect. Their efforts to defend these sacred sites, despite constant dangers and political challenges, illustrate their deep devotion and spiritual commitment. Their sacrifices to maintain Christianity in these symbolic places continue to fascinate and inspire, adding a layer of mystery to their legacy.

Dive into a world where faith and war intertwine, where the Templars, with their distinctive cross, were much more than just warriors: they were the guardians of the deepest secrets of Christianity. What drove these men to give up everything to protect pilgrims in the Holy Land? What treasures and knowledge did they accumulate over the centuries?

The mysteries surrounding the Templars are not limited to their lives and battles. Their secret rituals, codes, and hidden alliances continue to raise questions. Why were they so suddenly arrested and persecuted? What happened to their immense wealth and sacred archives?

This book is an invitation to discover not only the history of the Templars, but also the myths and realities that have shaped their legend.

From the foundation of the order to the tragic dissolution, each page will bring you closer to these men whose dedication and mystery have never ceased to intrigue.

The Templars, beyond their role as protectors of pilgrims, were also financiers and builders. Their economic influence was such that they owned lands, commanderies and even fabulous treasures that still arouse fantasies today. Rumours speak of the True Cross, the Holy Grail and secret manuscripts held by the order. The quest for these lost treasures continues to fascinate historians and adventurers.

The mysteries related to the fall of the Templars are just as intriguing. How could such a powerful organization be dismantled so quickly? Were the accusations of heresy and occult practices founded, or was it a plot to seize their wealth?

This book is aimed at all those who are fascinated by historical mysteries and stories of courage and devotion. Allow yourself to be drawn into a quest for truth, where each page reveals a new aspect of the life of the Templars, these enigmatic knights who have left an indelible mark on history.

The quest for answers will lead you through captivating narratives of epic battles, archaeological discoveries, and modern investigations attempting to unravel the secrets of the Templars. You will explore the boldest theories and the most incredible legends surrounding this mystical order. Contemporary testimonies, historical evidence, and speculations intertwine to create a rich and fascinating picture of what the Templars really were.

By diving into this book, you will discover how the Templars influenced not only their time, but also the following centuries. Their legacy is manifested in traditions, rituals, and modern organizations that claim their spirit and ideals. Their heroic deeds, sacrifices, and secrets are all open doors to a past that is gone but never forgotten.

This book is not just a historical exploration; it's an invitation to reflect on the power of faith, devotion, and mystery. The Templars, through their actions and beliefs, remind us that history is often much more complex and mysterious than it appears.

Chapter 1: The Foundation of the Order.

Historical context of the Crusades.

The 12th century opens on a Europe in effervescence, where the Christian faith permeates every aspect of daily life. Religious fervour reaches its peak in a world where kingdoms are still young, often in conflict, and where chivalry begins to structure itself around codes of honour and service to God. It is in this context of intense piety, feudal rivalries and ecclesiastical reforms that the Crusades are born, these sanctified military expeditions aimed at retaking the holy places fallen into the hands of Muslims.

The Crusades find their origin in the desperate call of Byzantine Emperor Alexios I Komnenos, whose Eastern Empire is besieged by the Seljuk Turks. In 1095, at the Council of Clermont, Pope Urban II responds to this call by launching a call to crusade. Urban II, seeing in this expedition an opportunity to reunify Christianity under the banner of Rome and to divert Western lords from their internal quarrels, preaches fervently the necessity to liberate Jerusalem and the holy places. His call resonates deeply throughout Christian Europe, where the promise of remission of sins attracts nobles and peasants.

The religious climate of the time is deeply influenced by the idea of pilgrimage, an act of devotion and penance. Jerusalem, with its sacred sites, is the ultimate goal of Christian pilgrims. However, the road to the Holy City is fraught with dangers, with pilgrims regularly attacked and robbed by bandits and Muslim forces. The stories of pilgrims returning from the Holy Land evoke the splendour of the holy places and the difficulties of the journey, further fuelling the desire to protect and secure these sacred routes. It is in this context that the Order of the Hospitallers was created to provide care and protection to pilgrims. Originally founded as a hospital in Jerusalem to care for sick or injured pilgrims, this order quickly developed into a military and hospital force, dedicated to the safety and support of Christian travellers on these perilous routes.

The Council of Clermont marks the beginning of the First Crusade, an endeavour that attracts thousands of knights, peasants, and clerics, united by a common goal: to retake Jerusalem. The First Crusade is a series of events marked by resounding victories and terrible trials. In 1099, after a gruelling siege, the Crusaders take Jerusalem, inflicting a terrible massacre on the Muslim and Jewish defenders. The capture of Jerusalem is a resounding triumph for Christianity and establishes the first Latin states of the East.

These states, including the Kingdom of Jerusalem, the County of Edessa, the Principality of Antioch, and the County of Tripoli, are constantly threatened by the surrounding Muslim forces. The Crusader lords, although they have managed to establish Christian strongholds, are in perpetual struggle to maintain their territories. They face well-organized and determined armies and must also manage complex relations with the local non-Christian populations.

The defence of these territories becomes a priority, and the need for a permanent military force to protect the pilgrims and the inhabitants of the Latin states becomes evident. It is in this context of urgent necessity that the idea of religious military orders is born, of which the Templars will be the most emblematic.

The idea of a religious order of knights meets several needs. It allows to channel the military ardour of European knights into a sanctified cause, to ensure a permanent military presence in the Holy Land, and to provide a strict disciplinary structure to those who devote themselves to the protection of pilgrims and the defence of holy places. The fusion of monastic life and military life offers an ideal model of Christian chivalry, where service to God is achieved through the protection of the faithful.

This era is also marked by ecclesiastical reforms aimed at strengthening the authority of the Church and moralizing Christian life. Religious military orders, like the Templars, are supported by the Pope and ecclesiastical authorities, who see in them a way to channel chivalrous violence into a just and sanctified cause.

The Crusades, by mobilizing resources and men on an unprecedented scale, transform European society. They open up communication routes, promote cultural and economic exchanges, and stimulate a sense of Christian solidarity that transcends feudal borders. The Templars, through their role as protectors and warriors, embody this fusion of piety and martiality that characterizes the spirit of the Crusades.

Thus, the origin of the Order of the Templars is set in a rich and complex historical context, where faith, war and the need to protect pilgrims and holy places combine to give birth to one of the most famous and enigmatic institutions of the Middle Ages.

The Beginnings of the Order (1118).

In the year of grace 1118, under the sky of a Middle Ages steeped in faith and war, an order was born destined to become one of the most famous and enigmatic in history: the Order of the Poor Knights of Christ and the Temple of Solomon, soon to be called the Templars. The beginnings of this order find their roots in a historical context where Christianity, shaken and exalted by the crusades, sought to protect itself and strengthen its presence in the Holy Land.

The dawn of the 12th century was marked by the capture of Jerusalem in 1099 during the First Crusade. The crusaders, galvanized by intense religious fervour, had conquered the Holy City at the cost of fierce battles and immense sacrifices. But the victory, although resounding, did not bring the hoped-for peace. It was in this climate of constant peril that the idea of an order dedicated to the protection of pilgrims was born.

The idea germinated in the early 1110s, under the impetus of a French knight named Hugues de Payens, originally from the Champagne region. Hugues, accompanied by eight companions also driven by unwavering faith and a desire to serve, presented himself to King Baldwin II of Jerusalem in 1118. They proposed to establish a military order dedicated to the protection of pilgrims and the defence of Christian territories in the Holy Land.

Baudouin II, perceiving this proposal as a providential solution to the prevailing insecurity, accepted with enthusiasm. He offered them a part of his palace, located in Jerusalem on the ruins of Solomon's Temple, from which they derived their name: the Knights Templar. Settled in this emblematic place, the nine knights dedicated themselves to their mission with exemplary rigor and devotion.

Devotion and Admiration.

The life of the early Templars was marked by prayer, service, and the protection of pilgrims. They lived in community, sharing everything, renouncing material wealth and worldly pleasures. This iron discipline and unwavering dedication quickly earned them a reputation as pious and courageous knights.

The asceticism of the Templars was also a strategy of distinction. In a world where knights were often perceived as brutal and greedy, the Templars represented a new form of chivalry, where strength was put at the service of faith and the protection of the innocent. Their religious commitment set them apart from other warriors and elevated them to the rank of champions of Christianity.

Their commanderies were complex and well-organized structures, often fortified, including chapels, dormitories, refectories, stables, and barns. They served as logistical bases for operations in the Holy Land and as refuges for pilgrims. The efficient administration of these estates allowed the Templars to finance their military activities and support their fortresses in the Holy Land.

The early successes of the Templars and their unwavering devotion attracted attention and admiration. They quickly became a formidable force in the Latin states of the East, actively participating in battles and sieges. Their presence reassured pilgrims and residents, promising them protection and aid in times of danger.

Thus, in the span of a few years, the Templars went from a small brotherhood of nine knights to an influential and respected military and religious organization. Their mission of protecting pilgrims and defending Christian territories propelled them to the heart of the political and military issues of the Holy Land. Their ideals of devotion, courage, and discipline made them champions of the Christian faith, engraving their name in history with indelible ink.

The beginnings of the Order of the Templars, forged in trials and faith, laid the foundations of a chivalric epic that would mark the centuries to come. Their history, imbued with mysticism and bravery, continues to fascinate and inspire, reminding us of the power of ideals and the greatness of sacrifices for a cause deemed just and sacred.

The Support of Saint Bernard of Clairvaux.

The 12th century was a time of great upheavals and fervent religious aspirations. At the heart of this era, the bright star of Saint Bernard of Clairvaux illuminated the dark paths of faith and war. A major figure in Christianity, Bernard played a crucial role in the rise of the Templars, offering these devoted knights not only his spiritual support, but also a theological and moral legitimacy that cemented their place in history.

Saint Bernard of Clairvaux, a Cistercian monk of fervent piety and unparalleled eloquence, was already a revered figure throughout Christian Europe. Born in 1090 into a noble family in Burgundy, he entered the Citeaux Abbey in 1113, before founding the Clairvaux Abbey in 1115. His fiery sermons and inspired writings made him a powerful voice, capable of galvanizing crowds and advising the powerful.

Bernard's path crossed that of the Templars at a critical moment in their existence. Founded in 1118 by Hugues de Payens and eight knight companions, the Order of the Templars needed official recognition and institutional support to ensure its survival and development. Hugues de Payens, aware of the importance of such support, turned to Bernard of Clairvaux, whose influence in the papal court and ecclesiastical circles was immense.

Bernard, recognizing the potential of the Templars as defenders of Christianity and examples of chivalrous virtue, became their ardent defender. In 1129, at the Council of Troyes, he played a decisive role in the approval of the Templars' rule. His support helped to dispel the doubts and hesitations of other ecclesiastical dignitaries, convinced by Bernard's fervour and vision.

The Praise of the New Militia.

At the Council of Troyes, Bernard describes the Templars as warriors of God, who fight not for personal glory or material gain, but for justice and faith. He praises their austerity, their discipline, and their devotion, asserting that their mission transcends temporal values to reach the highest spiritual ideals. In his praise, Bernard writes: "They fight with a double sword, that of the body and that of the spirit, and bear the cross of Christ on their chest and on their shoulders."

This text, widely disseminated and read throughout Europe, plays a crucial role in the legitimization and popularization of the Templars. It attracts recruits from all social classes, seduced by the chivalrous ideal and the promise of sin remission for those who join the order. Donations pour in, commanderies multiply, and the influence of the Templars rapidly expands thanks to Bernard's blessing.

A Spiritual and Political Support.

Bernard de Clairvaux's support was not limited to inspiring writings. He also played a role as advisor and mediator, helping the Templars navigate the political and religious complexities of the time. His influence with popes and kings was crucial in ensuring the protection and growth of the order.

Bernard used his vast network of contacts to defend the interests of the Templars and secure privileges for them. He persuaded Pope Innocent II to place the order directly under papal authority, thus ensuring their independence from local bishops and feudal lords. This papal protection allowed them to act freely, without the constraints of local rivalries, and to fully devote themselves to their mission.

Furthermore, Bernard played a crucial role in the organization of the Crusades, encouraging the participation of European knights and lords. He passionately preached the Second Crusade, urging the faithful to take up the cross and join the Templars in their holy struggle. His charisma and conviction led thousands of crusaders across Europe, strengthening the ranks of the Templars and consolidating their central role in military expeditions to the Holy Land.

A Spiritual Symbiosis.

The link between Bernard of Clairvaux and the Templars went far beyond logistical and political support. Bernard saw in them an extension of his own monastic vision, an order that combined the spiritual rigor of the Cistercians with the martial bravery of the knights. This fusion of contemplative and active life embodied the Christian ideal, where the spirit and the body worked together for the glory of God.

The Templars, for their part, found in Bernard a source of inspiration and spiritual guidance. His writings, sermons, and letters became fundamental texts for the order, guiding their actions and prayers. The Cistercian spirituality, centred on contemplation, simplicity, and total devotion to God, permeated the life of the Templars, giving them a spiritual depth that transcended their military mission.

A Lasting Legacy.

The support of Bernard de Clairvaux had lasting repercussions on the order of the Templars. Thanks to his backing, they became not only a formidable military force, but also a respected and revered institution throughout Christendom.

Today, the legacy of Bernard de Clairvaux endures, not only in the history of the Templars, but also in the history of Christianity. His vision of a knighthood devoted to God and justice continues to inspire, reminding us that even in the darkest moments, faith and devotion can illuminate the path. Through his support, Bernard de Clairvaux gave the

Templars the wings they needed to rise above mere human quarrels and become the sacred guardians of the Christian faith.

The Official Recognition by the Pope.

The Templars, this group, humble in its beginnings but grandiose in its vision, would soon receive recognition that would change its destiny forever. The year 1129 was that of the official consecration of the Templars by the papacy, a moment of divine light in the annals of Christian history.

Hugues de Payens, the first master of the order, knew that for the Templars to fully fulfil their mission, they needed greater support than that of kings and nobles. They needed the blessing and protection of the Church itself. With unwavering determination, he travelled to Europe to plead the cause of his order to the highest ecclesiastical dignitaries. His journey culminated in 1127, when he appeared before the Council of Troyes, convened by Pope Honorius II.

The Council of Troyes, which was held in January 1129, brought together the most eminent clerics and lords of the time. Bernard of Clairvaux, the spiritual soul of the Cistercians and one of the most influential ecclesiastics of the time, played a crucial role in the recognition of the Templars.

This is how Bernard of Clairvaux wrote a text entitled "De Laude Novae Militiae" (In Praise of the New Knighthood), a treatise extolling the virtues of the Templars and justifying their existence in the eyes of the Church and the Christian world. In this text, Bernard did not just defend the Templars; he elevated them to an almost divine status, describing them as soldiers of Christ, fighting the forces of evil with religious fervour and exemplary military discipline.

The Council of Troyes began in an atmosphere charged with expectations and solemnity. Hugues de Payens, dressed in the white habit of the Templars, humbly presented himself before the assembly, but his voice carried the strength of an unwavering conviction. He explained the mission of the order, its necessity in a world plagued by insecurity, and the urgent need for the protection of pilgrims. He also described the strict rules of the order, based on the precepts of Saint Benedict, but adapted to the life of a knight.

The discussions were intense. The bishops and abbots weighed the arguments, analysed the risks and benefits of such a military order under the auspices of the Church. Bernard of Clairvaux, with his charisma and wisdom, played a decisive role in calming doubts and strengthening convictions. He argued that the Templars, through their dedication and discipline, could serve as a bulwark against the forces of evil, while inspiring European chivalry to follow their example of piety and courage.

After days of deliberation, the Council of Troyes made a decision that would resonate through the ages. On January 13, 1129, the Templars were officially recognized by the Church. The rule of the order, largely written by Bernard of Clairvaux, was approved. This rule established the foundations of their monastic and military life: poverty, chastity, obedience, and an unwavering commitment to the defence of pilgrims and holy places.

The papal recognition of the Templars had immediate and profound repercussions. It conferred upon the order a spiritual legitimacy and a moral authority that allowed it to grow and prosper. The Templars were no longer mere wandering knights; they were now sacred warriors, invested with a divine mission. This recognition attracted donations and lands from nobles and kings eager to support the Christian cause. Templar commanderies multiplied, becoming centres of power and resources.

The papal blessing also protected the Templars from secular ambitions. By being placed directly under the authority of the Pope, they escaped feudal rivalries and the greed of local lords. This independence allowed them to carry out their mission without hindrance, enhancing their effectiveness and dedication.

Pope Honorius II, in granting his blessing, also saw in the Templars a providential instrument to maintain Christianity in the Holy

Land. The Latin states, fragile and constantly threatened, needed tireless and incorruptible defenders. The Templars, through their courage and faith, were the ideal champions of this sacred cause.

The years following the official recognition saw the order of the Templars structure and strengthen itself. Their rule, strict and austere, ensured an iron discipline. The Templar knights became a military elite, respected and feared, wearing their red cross on their white coats as a symbol of their devotion to the cause of Christ.

This recognition was not just an administrative act; it was a sacrament, a sanctification of their mission. The Templars, now invested with a divine mission, devoted themselves body and soul to the protection of pilgrims and the defence of the Holy Land. Their unwavering faith and unparalleled bravery propelled them to the heart of battles and sieges, where their presence could make the difference between life and death, between victory and defeat.

Thus, the official recognition by the Pope in 1129 marked the beginning of a golden era for the Templars. It was a divine blessing, a legitimization of their sacred mission. The Knights Templar, armed with their faith and courage, wrote pages of history in letters of blood and fire, becoming the guardians of the holy places and the protectors of the pilgrims.

Mission and objectives of the Templars.

The primary mission of the Templars, as envisioned by their founding knights, is to protect pilgrims in the Holy Land. The pilgrimage to Jerusalem, a high place of Christianity, is an act of faith and penance. However, the roads leading to the holy places are fraught with pitfalls: bandits roam, Muslim forces are omnipresent, and dangers of all kinds threaten travellers. The Templars dedicate themselves to this noble task of protection, arming their arm and heart to defend the faithful against the perils of the journey.

To successfully carry out this mission, the Templars adopt an austere and communal way of life. Their commitment is manifested by three solemn vows: poverty, chastity, and obedience. By renouncing material wealth, they embrace a life of simplicity, where every possession is put at the service of their mission. Chastity, for its part, purifies their devotion, detaching them from worldly temptations to fully dedicate themselves to their sacred cause. Finally, obedience ensures discipline and unity within the order, each knight submitting to the authority of his superiors and to the rule of the order.

The defence of the Latin states of the East, born from the Crusades, becomes a crucial objective for the Templars. These territories, fragments of Christianity in Muslim land, are constantly threatened by hostile forces. The Templars erect and fortify castles, fortresses and bastions at strategic points, thus forming a defensive network intended to repel enemy assaults. Their fortresses, such as those of Tortosa, Safed, and the famous Krak des Chevaliers, become symbols of resistance and determination.

But the Templars are not content to passively defend these bastions. They lead daring military expeditions, actively participating in battles and sieges. Their courage and discipline set them apart on the battlefields. The red cross adorning their white coats becomes a symbol of bravery and sacrifice. Their chivalrous charges, often decisive, earn them a formidable reputation among the fighters of the time.

Beyond the protection of pilgrims and the defence of territories, the Templars embrace a profound spiritual goal: the defence of the Christian faith. They perceive themselves as the champions of Christianity, ready to sacrifice their lives for the glory of God and the salvation of souls. Their spiritual commitment is manifested in their daily prayers, their religious rites, and their constant devotion. Each battle is perceived not only as an earthly fight, but as a divine struggle against the forces of evil.

The mission of the Templars also extends to the administration and management of vast estates in Europe and the East. Their commanderies, scattered throughout the Christian kingdoms, become centres of economic and social activity. The Templars cultivate lands, raise livestock, and engage in commercial activities. The revenues generated by these activities allow them to finance their military expeditions and support their fortresses in the Holy Land.

In addition to their agricultural and commercial activities, the Templars develop advanced banking services for the time. They secure the funds of pilgrims and nobles, facilitate money transfers, and grant loans. Their reputation for integrity and reliability makes them trusted partners for kings and lords, thus consolidating their economic and political influence.

The Templars also aim to promote justice and peace. In a world marked by feudal conflicts and power struggles, they intervene as mediators and protectors of the weak. Their code of conduct, based on the principles of chivalry and righteousness, guides their actions and inspires respect. They defend the oppressed, protect orphans and widows, and support local Christian communities.

The education and training of young knights is another important objective for the Templars. They welcome and train novices, teaching them not only martial arts and military tactics, but also the values of the order: piety, honour, and service. The young recruits learn to handle weapons, ride horses, and behave like true Christian knights. This rigorous training ensures the continuity of the order and the transmission of its ideals through generations.

Finally, the Templars nurture the hope of reconquering Jerusalem. Despite setbacks and defeats, their ultimate goal remains the liberation of the holy places and the restoration of the Christian kingdom of Jerusalem. Each expedition, each battle, each act of bravery is imbued with this ideal. The cross of Jerusalem, symbol of their sacred mission, guides their steps and inspires their determination.

Chapter 2: The Rise of the Templars.

The Rule of the Templars.

The rule of the Templars, both strict and inspired, was the fundamental charter that guided every aspect of the knights' lives, from their martial actions to their spiritual devotion.

Composed of 72 articles, it begins with a preface extolling the ideal of Christian chivalry. It emphasizes that the Knights of the Temple must be champions of faith, defenders of the poor and pilgrims, and soldiers of God in the fight against the infidels.

Monastic Life and Spiritual Commitments.

At the heart of the rule, lie the three fundamental monastic vows: poverty, chastity, and obedience. These vows, borrowed from the Benedictine tradition, are adapted to the military vocation of the Templars. Poverty, first of all, is a commitment to renounce material wealth. The knights own nothing themselves, each asset being pooled to serve the mission of the order. This voluntary poverty symbolizes their detachment from earthly goods and their total dependence on divine providence.

Chastity, for its part, requires the Templars to lead a life of continence, distancing them from worldly distractions and temptations. By renouncing marriage and carnal relations, they dedicate their energy and spirit to God and the sacred cause of the order. This purity of body and soul is perceived as a spiritual weapon, strengthening their determination and devotion.

Obedience, finally, is the cornerstone of Templar discipline. Each knight submits to the authority of his superiors and to the rule of the order. This submission is not a simple hierarchical subordination, but an expression of trust and loyalty towards the common mission. Obedience ensures the cohesion and effectiveness of the order, allowing perfect coordination on the battlefields and in the management of commanderies.

Daily Life and Discipline.

The Templars' rule also details the daily life of the knights, blending military rigor and monastic asceticism. The days start early, with morning prayers followed by mass. Prayer is omnipresent, marking every moment of the day. Religious services punctuate their existence, constantly reminding them of their devotion to God.

The meals are frugal, composed mainly of bread, vegetables, and lean meat. Silence is mandatory during meals, allowing the knights to meditate and reflect. Meals are taken communally, reinforcing the spirit of fraternity and equality among them. The sobriety of the table is a constant reminder of their commitment to poverty and discipline.

The clothing of the Templars is also regulated. They wear a white tunic, symbol of purity, adorned with the red cross, sign of their sacred commitment. The clothes are simple and functional, adapted to the rigors of military campaigns. The armours and weapons are kept in perfect condition, each knight being responsible for his equipment, symbol of his constant readiness for battle.

Leisure times are rare and devoted to useful activities: weapon maintenance, martial training, or manual labour. Knights must be ready to go on a mission at any time, living in a state of constant vigilance. Rigorous training ensures their effectiveness on the battlefield, while manual labour reminds them of their commitment to a simple and laborious life.

Governance and Hierarchy.

The rule of the Templars establishes a strict hierarchy, ensuring effective governance and iron discipline. At the head of the order is the grand master, elected by his peers and invested with supreme authority. He is assisted by a seneschal, a marshal, a land commander, and a draper, each with specific responsibilities. The seneschal oversees the general administration of the order, the marshal is responsible for military affairs, the land commander manages territorial possessions, and the draper takes care of clothing and equipment.

Important decisions are made in chapter, an assembly where higher-ranking knights discuss and deliberate on the affairs of the order. Transparency and collegiality are essential principles, with each decision subject to collective approval. This hierarchical structure ensures orderly management and allows for a quick and coordinated response to military and administrative challenges.

The knights must obey their superiors without hesitation. This obedience is perceived as an act of faith, each order being executed in the spirit of service to God. The punishments for breaking the rule are severe, ranging from penance to banishment. The rigorous discipline maintains the cohesion and reputation of the order, ensuring that each knight embodies the values of the order.

Military and Sacred Devotion.

The military mission of the Templars is at the heart of their rule. They are defenders of the faith, tasked with protecting pilgrims and defending Christian lands against infidels. Their martial training is intensive, each knight being trained in the handling of weapons, tactics and military strategy. Discipline on the battlefield is relentless, each knight knowing that he must fight with courage and loyalty, ready to sacrifice his life for the cause.

The rule of the Templars does not just regulate the material and spiritual life of the knights; it shapes an identity, an ethos. Each knight is a soldier of Christ, his entire life dedicated to the fight against evil and the protection of the innocent. The red cross on their tunic is more than a symbol; it's an oath, a promise of loyalty to God and the order.

The Templars are also builders. They construct fortresses, churches, and hospitals, ensuring the safety and well-being of Christian communities. Their presence reassures pilgrims and residents, promising protection and assistance when needed. Each commandery is a bastion of faith and strength, a refuge in an often hostile world.

The Rapid Expansion and Establishment of Commanderies.

The Templars, thanks to a combination of fervent faith, military discipline, and ecclesiastical support, experienced a rapid expansion that would deeply mark medieval history. Their establishment of commanderies across Europe and the Levant became the backbone of their power and influence.

The Commanderies: Centres of Power and Faith.

The Templar commanderies quickly become multifunctional structures, serving as both military bases, administrative centres and refuges for pilgrims. Each commandery is designed according to a rigorous plan, reflecting the discipline and order that characterize the Templars. They generally include a chapel, dormitories, refectories, stables, workshops and fortifications.

The chapel is the spiritual heart of every commandery. Here, the knights gather to pray, attend mass, and meditate. The simplicity and sobriety of these buildings reflect their devotion and vow of poverty. The dormitories, on the other hand, are austere resting places, where each knight has a spartan cell, reminding them of their commitment to chastity and discipline. The refectories, where meals are taken in common, are places of sharing and fraternity. Silence is often the rule, allowing the knights to meditate and reflect. The stables and workshops are the centres of practical activities. The Templars maintain their horses, manufacture and repair their weapons and equipment. Martial discipline and rigorous training are essential aspects of daily life, preparing the knights for battles and dangerous missions.

Geographic and Strategic Expansion.

The expansion of the Templar commanderies is not limited to the Holy Land. Thanks to generous donations and the support of the Church, the Templars establish commanderies throughout Europe. These establishments become nerve centres of Templar power, facilitating communications, travel, and fundraising to support their activities in the East.

In France, the cradle of the order, the commanderies multiply rapidly. Regions such as Burgundy, Champagne and Provence become Templar strongholds, housing some of the most powerful and wealthy commanderies. The fertile lands and agricultural estates allow the Templars to generate substantial revenues, which they reinvest in the defence of the Holy Land and the maintenance of their infrastructure.

In England, the Templars find enthusiastic support from kings and nobles. The English commanderies, well-managed and prosperous, play a crucial role in financing the Crusades. Cities like London and York become important centres for the Templars, who establish solid bases there.

In Spain and Portugal, the Templars actively participate in the Reconquista, the effort to retake the Iberian Peninsula from the Moors. Their military commitment and their expertise in fortification contribute to many Christian victories. The Iberian commanderies, in addition to their spiritual and military functions, also serve as gathering points for the crusades to the Holy Land.

Administration and Governance.

Each commandery is led by a commander, chosen for his experience and loyalty. The commander is responsible for daily management, discipline and training of the knights, as well as the administration of lands and resources. He reports directly to the provincial master, who oversees several commanderies in a given region.

The governance of the commanderies relies on a strict hierarchy and efficient administration. The Templars develop advanced management methods, keeping detailed records of their possessions, their income, and their expenses. This administrative rigor allows them to maximize their resources and effectively support their missions in the Holy Land.

The income of the commanderies comes from various sources: agriculture, livestock, crafts, and sometimes even banking activities. The Templars develop sophisticated financial services, securing the funds of pilgrims and nobles, facilitating money transfers and granting loans. Their reputation for integrity and reliability makes them trusted partners for financial transactions.

Military and Defensive Role.

Commanderies are not only economic and spiritual centres; they also play a crucial role in the defence of Christian territories. Fortified and strategically located, they serve as bastions against enemy incursions. The knights, well-trained and disciplined, are ready to defend their lands and respond to calls for help from the Latin states of the East.

In the Holy Land, the commanderies are rallying points for the crusading troops. The Templars build and maintain imposing fortresses, like the Krak des Chevaliers in Syria, symbol of their power and determination. These fortresses, equipped with garrisons and reserves, allow the Templars to sustain prolonged sieges and launch counterattacks against the Muslim forces.

Social and Political Impact.

The influence of the Templar commanderies extends beyond military and economic aspects. They become local power centres, involved in the social and political affairs of the regions where they are established. The Templars, respected for their integrity and dedication, often play a role as mediators and protectors of the weak. They defend the rights of peasants, protect orphans and widows, and support local Christian communities.

Their involvement in local affairs strengthens their reputation and legitimacy. The local populations, seeing them as fair defenders and competent administrators, grant them their support and loyalty. This positive interaction with local communities contributes to the stability and prosperity of regions under Templar influence.

The rapid expansion and establishment of the Templar commanderies are testimonies to the vision and determination of the Templars. Within a few decades, they transform a modest group of knights into a powerful and respected organization, present throughout Europe and the Levant. The commanderies, centres of faith, discipline, and power, become the pillars of this expansion, supporting the military and spiritual missions of the order.

Their network of commanderies, far beyond simple fortresses, symbolizes a unique fusion of faith and chivalry, a legacy that continues to inspire and fascinate through the ages.

Chapter 3: The Organization and Life within the Order.

Hierarchical Structure of the Templars.

The Order of the Poor Knights of Christ and the Temple of Solomon, better known as the Templars, was organized according to a rigorous and methodical hierarchical structure. This internal organization, both complex and precise, was essential for maintaining discipline and efficiency within the order, both on the battlefield and within their commanderies. The hierarchy of the Templars, inspired by both military and monastic principles, ensured effective governance and unwavering cohesion among the knights.

The Grand Master.

At the top of the Templar hierarchy was the Grand Master, the most eminent and respected figure of the order. The Grand Master was elected by the general chapter, composed of the highest-ranking members of the order, including provincial commanders and the most influential knights. This election often took place after intensive deliberations, where the wisdom, military experience, and religious devotion of the candidates were carefully evaluated.

The Grand Master held supreme authority within the order, overseeing all military, administrative, and spiritual activities. He was responsible for military strategy, diplomatic relations with kings and popes, and managing the order's resources. The Grand Master also represented the Templars at ecclesiastical councils and political assemblies, playing a crucial role in defending the interests of the order.

The Seneschal.

Immediately under the Grand Master was the Seneschal, his main deputy and advisor. The Seneschal was in charge of the internal administration of the order, ensuring that the commanderies functioned efficiently and that the directives of the Grand Master were implemented. He coordinated daily activities, managed finances, and oversaw logistics. In the absence of the Grand Master, the Seneschal assumed his duties, thus ensuring a continuity of command.

The Marshal.

The Marshal was the military leader of the order, responsible for the training, equipment, and discipline of the knights. He organized military campaigns, planned battles, and led the Templar forces on the battlefield. The Marshal had to possess exceptional expertise in military strategy and an ability to inspire and lead men. Under his command, the knights trained rigorously and prepared for the most perilous missions.

The Commander of the Earth and the Draper.

Two other important figures completed the summit of the Templar hierarchy: the Commander of the Land and the Draper. The Commander of the Land was responsible for managing the order's land possessions. He oversaw the operation of agricultural lands, vineyards, and livestock, ensuring that the revenues generated were used to finance the order's activities. The Draper, on the other hand, oversaw the supply of clothing, armour, and equipment. He ensured that each knight had the necessary equipment to carry out his mission.

The Provincial Commanders.

Beneath the Grand Master and his council were the Provincial Commanders, who governed the different provinces of the order. Each province, or bailiwick, corresponded to a specific geographical region, often a country or a large region of it. The Provincial Commanders were responsible for the administration and defence of their province, as well as the supervision of local commanderies. They reported directly to the Grand Master and the Seneschal.

The Commanders of Commandries.

The commanderies, or Templar houses, were led by Commanders of the Commandery. These commanderies could vary in size, ranging from simple fortified farms to vast complexes including chapels, dormitories, refectories, and fortifications. The Commander of the

Commandery managed the daily affairs of the commandery, overseeing agricultural, craft, and commercial activities. He was also responsible for the training and discipline of the knights and sergeants stationed in his commandery.

The Knights and the Sergeants.

The Templar knights, nobles by birth, constituted the military elite of the order. Trained in martial arts and military tactics, they wore the distinctive Templar attire: a white tunic adorned with a red cross. Their lives were punctuated by prayer, training, and military missions. The knights lived according to a strict rule, respecting the vows of poverty, chastity, and obedience.

Alongside the knights were the sergeants, often from lower social classes but just as devoted. The sergeants played a crucial role in the order, fulfilling military and administrative functions. On the battlefield, they fought alongside the knights, forming an essential auxiliary force. In the commanderies, they could hold positions of responsibility, ensuring the smooth running of daily operations.

The Chaplains and the Lay Brothers.

The chaplains, members of the clergy, were integrated into the order to take care of the spiritual needs of the knights and sergeants. They celebrated mass, administered the sacraments, and offered spiritual advice. Their presence was vital to maintain religious fervour and moral discipline within the order.

The lay brothers, for their part, were non-combatant members who supported the activities of the order through their work. They oversaw agricultural, craft and administrative tasks, allowing the knights and sergeants to focus on their military and spiritual missions.

The General Chapter.

The General Chapter was the supreme decision-making body of the order, meeting periodically to deliberate on important issues and elect the Grand Master. Composed of the highest dignitaries of the order, including the Provincial Commanders and the principal officers, the General Chapter made strategic decisions and ensured the cohesion and unity of the order. Discussions were conducted with solemnity and seriousness, each decision being made in the spirit of service to God and the mission of the Templars.

Discipline and Sanctions.

Discipline within the order was rigorously maintained. Breaches of the rule or acts of disobedience were severely punished. Sanctions could range from simple penance to expulsion from the order. This strict discipline was essential to preserve the integrity and effectiveness of the order, ensuring that each member remained faithful to their vows and their mission.

Conclusion.

The hierarchical structure of the Templars was a masterful fusion of military discipline and monastic devotion. Each level of this hierarchy played a crucial role in the governance and effectiveness of the order. From the Grand Master to the lay brothers, each member was united by a common mission and a strict rule of life, forging an order that left an indelible mark on medieval history. This rigorous organization allowed the Templars to become a formidable and respected force, devoted to the protection of holy places and the defence of the Christian faith.

Daily Life of the Knights Templar.

In past centuries, behind the austere walls of the commanderies, the rigorously regulated life of the Knights Templar unfolded. These men, bound by vows of poverty, chastity, and obedience, led a life where each day was a quest for devotion, discipline, and military preparation. Their daily life, far from the romantic images of feasts and constant battles, was marked by monastic austerity and unwavering commitment to their sacred mission.

The Dawn of the Day: Prayer and Meditation.

The day began before dawn, in the silent darkness of the Templar chapels. The knights rose to the sound of the bell, a call to the first prayer of the day. Gathered in the chapel, they recited matins, the first of the eight canonical hours. These prayers, sung or recited in chorus, structured the day and constantly reminded the knights of their devotion to God. Prayer was a moment of reflection, meditation and spiritual communion, an essential preparation to face the trials of the day.

The Mass and the Refreshment.

After matins, the knights attended mass, celebrated by the chaplain of the commandery. The daily mass was a central pillar of their spiritual life, a moment when they renewed their commitment and drew the necessary divine strength for their mission. Communion, a symbol of union with Christ, was a sacred act that strengthened their faith and determination.

Following the mass, came the refreshment, the first meal of the day. Taken in silence in the refectory, this meal was frugal and simple, often composed of bread, cheese, vegetables and water. Silence was respected to allow meditation and listening to pious readings, often passages from the Bible or writings of saints. This communal meal strengthened the bonds of brotherhood and reminded the knights of their commitment to poverty and discipline.

Military Training and Practical Work.

After the meal, the day continued with physical and military activities. The knights engaged in rigorous training sessions, handling weapons, combat exercises and equestrian practices. Mastery of the sword, lance, and bow was essential, as was physical endurance and battle strategy. The knights prepared tirelessly for the upcoming battles, aware that their military effectiveness was crucial for the defence of the holy places and pilgrims.

In addition to military training, the knights participated in the practical work necessary for the smooth running of the commandery.

They could be involved in agricultural tasks, such as land cultivation and vineyard maintenance, or in craft activities, such as blacksmithing and carpentry. These tasks, far from their noble status, were an expression of their vow of poverty and a means of contributing to the Templar community.

The Midday Prayer and the Meal.

At noon, the bell rang again for the hour of sext prayer. The knights interrupted their activities to gather again in the chapel. This prayer, like those at dawn, was a reminder of their constant devotion and a spiritual break in the middle of the day.

After prayer, the knights would have their second meal, similar in simplicity to the morning repast. Silence was once again mandatory, allowing for the reading of the Scriptures and personal reflection. This moment of rest was brief, as the knights quickly returned to their military or practical duties.

The Afternoon: Continuity of Activities.

The afternoon was dedicated to the continuation of the morning's activities. The knights were perfecting their martial skills, strengthening the fortifications, maintaining their mounts, and overseeing the work of the commandery. The discipline was strict, each knight being responsible for his equipment and personal preparation. The commanderies, true fortresses, had to be ready at any moment to repel attacks or to set off on an expedition.

Administrative activities were also part of the afternoon. The heads of the commanderies kept precise records of resources, finances, and operations. The knights involved in managing the order's lands and assets ensured that everything was in order, thus ensuring the prosperity and self-sufficiency of the community.

Vespers and Compline.

At the end of the afternoon, the knights would gather again for vespers, the evening prayer. This moment of reflection marked the transition between daily activities and spiritual preparation for the night. The songs and prayers of vespers were a tribute to divine greatness and a call for divine protection for the coming night.

Before retiring, the knights recited the compline, the last prayer of the day. This prayer, more intimate and personal, was an opportunity to ask for forgiveness for the sins committed, to thank God for his blessings, and to seek inner peace. The compline ended the day, leaving the knights in a state of serenity and spiritual readiness.

The Night: Vigil and Rest.

At nightfall, the knights would retreat to their dormitories, simple and austere cells, reminding them of their vow of poverty. Rest was short and often interrupted by vigils of prayer or guard duty. The knights, even in sleep, had to remain ready to respond to any threat or call for help.

The vigil was an essential element of their daily life. The knights alternated guard shifts, monitoring the fortifications and ensuring the safety of the commandery. This constant vigilance was a manifestation of their dedication and their readiness to defend Christendom at any moment.

The Brotherhood and Community Life.

The daily life of the Templar knights was also marked by a strong community dimension. Brotherhood and solidarity were at the heart of their existence. The knights lived, prayed, ate and fought together, forging bonds of camaraderie and unwavering loyalty.

The moments of relaxation, although rare, were spent together, strengthening the team spirit and unity. The discussions, simple games and exchanges of experiences created an environment where each knight could count on the support and understanding of his brothers in arms. This solidarity was crucial, especially in the face of the constant trials and dangers of their mission.

Conclusion.

The daily life of the Knights Templar, far from heroic images of epic battles, was an existence of austerity, discipline, and devotion. Each day, structured by prayer, work, and training, was a constant quest for spiritual and military perfection. The knights, uniting monastic life with warrior life, embodied an ideal of Christian chivalry where faith and duty merged into a sacred mission. Their unwavering commitment and austere lifestyle leave a lasting imprint in history, symbolizing the union of piety and bravery in the service of God and Christendom.

Rituals and Religious Practices of the Knights Templar.

In the mystery and solemnity of the Gothic chapels, the Templar knights, armed with their unwavering faith and unfailing devotion, performed rituals and religious practices that structured their existence and fortified their spirit. These ceremonies, imbued with symbolism and devotion, were much more than simple liturgical obligations; they were the spiritual foundations of their sacred mission.

The Daily Mass.

At the heart of the Templars' religious life was the daily mass, celebrated every morning at dawn. The chant of matins echoed in the cold stones of the chapels, marking the beginning of a new day dedicated to God. The knights, dressed in their white habit adorned with the red cross, gathered in silence, their heads bowed in prayer.

The mass, celebrated by the chaplain of the commandery, was a moment of profound spiritual communion. The prayers and Gregorian chants rose to the heavens, carrying praises and supplications. The liturgy of the Word, with readings from the Scriptures and homilies, nourished their faith and provided teachings to guide their daily actions. The consecration of the Eucharist, a sacred mystery where the bread and wine became the body and blood of Christ, was the climax of the mass. In receiving communion, the knights renewed their commitment to follow in the footsteps of Christ, ready to sacrifice their lives for the defence of the faith.

The Canonical Hours.

The prayers of the canonical hours marked the day of the Templars, uniting their souls in a symphony of devotion. The rule of the order required the knights to pray eight times a day, following the ancient monastic offices of the liturgy of the hours: matins, lauds, prime, terce, sext, none, vespers and compline. Each office had its own significance, recalling the key moments in the life of Christ and the saints.

The matins, the first prayer of the day, were sung in the freshness of dawn, an offering of the early hours to God. The lauds, celebrated at sunrise, were songs of praise for the renewed creation. Prime, terce, sext, and none, prayed throughout the day, sanctified the work and activities of the knights, reminding that every action should be performed in honour of God. The vespers, sung at dusk, thanked God for the blessings of the day and implored his protection for the night. The compline, the last prayer before rest, asked for forgiveness for the faults committed and a peaceful night under divine guard.

The Monastic Vows.

The rituals of taking vows were solemn moments where knights publicly committed to follow the precepts of poverty, chastity, and obedience. These vows, inspired by Benedictine and Cistercian rules, were the cornerstone of their religious life. The ceremony of taking vows often took place in front of the master of the commandery and the assembled brothers.

The knight pronounced his vows with his hands placed on the Bible, promising to renounce material possessions, to live in purity, and to submit to the authority of his superiors. The consecration was sealed by the reception of the Templar habit: the white tunic and the cloak adorned with the red cross. This habit, a symbol of their commitment and purity, was worn with pride and humility.

The General and Provincial Chapters.

The general and provincial chapters were assemblies where the knights would gather to discuss the affairs of the order, make important decisions, and renew their commitment. These meetings, held in a setting of prayer and meditation, always began with religious services, invoking divine wisdom to guide their deliberations.

The chapters were moments of great solemnity, where each knight could express his concerns and suggestions. The decisions made during these meetings were often preceded by periods of fasting and prayer, reflecting the importance of the issues debated. The ritual of collective confession, where each knight confessed his shortcomings before his brothers, reinforced cohesion and humility within the order.

The Pilgrimages.

Pilgrimages were an essential part of the Templars' spirituality. These journeys to holy places, particularly to Jerusalem, were acts of deep devotion, symbolizing the spiritual journey of each knight. Pilgrimages offered opportunities to renew faith, seek forgiveness, and meditate on divine mysteries.

The rituals surrounding pilgrimages included specific prayers, blessings before departure, and acts of penance throughout the journey. Upon their arrival at the holy places, the knights would prostrate themselves in prayer, often at the foot of the Holy Sepulchre, imploring divine grace and mercy. These moments of piety strengthened their determination and commitment to defend these sacred places.

The Funeral and the Memory.

The funeral rituals of the Templars were imbued with dignity and respect. Death, seen as a transition to eternal life, was celebrated with solemn services and prayers for the rest of the deceased's soul. The knights, in their white habit, followed the coffin in procession, singing psalms and hymns of comfort.

The graves were often simple, marked by the Templar cross. The chapels of the commanderies sometimes housed the tombs of the knights, reminding of their sacrifice and dedication. Requiem services, regularly celebrated, honoured the memory of the deceased, praying for their soul and reaffirming the spiritual solidarity between the living and the dead.

The Holidays and Solemnities.

The liturgical feasts and solemnities were moments of joy and celebration within the order. Christmas, Easter, and the feasts of the patron saints of the Templars, such as Saint Bernard of Clairvaux, were marked by solemn masses, processions and communal banquets. These celebrations, although joyful, were always imbued with piety and respect, reminding of the sacred nature of their mission.

Conclusion.

The rituals and religious practices of the Knights Templar, meticulously observed and deeply respected, formed the spiritual framework of their existence. Each prayer, each ceremony, each act of devotion was an affirmation of their unwavering faith and total commitment to God. Through these sacred rites, the Templars found the strength, inspiration, and serenity needed to fulfil their mission in a world of tumult and danger. Their lives, rooted in rigorous spirituality, reflected an unceasing quest for holiness and service, leaving a lasting imprint in the history of Christianity.

Chapter 4: The Military Campaigns.

Participation in the Crusades: The Key Role of the Templars in the Crusades.

In the clash of arms and the cry of battles, the Templar knights stood as living ramparts of Christendom, their red crosses shimmering in the Holy Land's sun. From the first crusades, the Order of the Poor Knights of Christ and of the Temple of Solomon distinguished itself by its indomitable courage and fervent devotion. Their participation in the crusades was not only an expression of their faith, but also a testament to their commitment to defending the holy places against the forces seeking to destroy them.

The First Crusade and the Foundation of the Order.

Although the Order of the Templars was only founded after the first crusade, the roots of their military vocation plunge into this tumultuous era. In 1099, the capture of Jerusalem by the crusaders marked a decisive turning point in the history of Christianity. The first crusaders, under the banner of God, had liberated the Holy City from Muslim hands, but the path of the pilgrims remained fraught with dangers. It was in this context that the idea of an order of knights dedicated to the protection of pilgrims took shape, leading to the creation of the Templars in 1119 by Hugues de Payens and his companions.

The First Crusade, preached by Pope Urban II in 1095, was a response to the desperate calls of the Byzantines, threatened by the expansion of the Seljuk Turks. Urban II, in his fiery speech at the Council of Clermont, called on Western Christians to take up arms to defend the faith and liberate Jerusalem. This call resonated deeply in European hearts, sparking a massive and varied movement of nobles and commoners, all determined to respond to this divine call.

The Crusaders, after a gruelling journey through Europe and Asia Minor, finally reached Jerusalem in 1099. The conquest of the city, although marked by extreme violence, was seen as a miraculous victory. The Crusaders had accomplished the unthinkable, but their task was far from over. The surrounding territories were still under Muslim control, and the safety of Christian pilgrims traveling to the Holy Land was constantly threatened by bands of looters and residual enemy forces.

The Second Crusade.

The Second Crusade (1147-1149) was the first major conflict in which the Templars actively participated. The call to arms was launched by Pope Eugene III after the fall of Edessa, one of the Latin states of the East, into the hands of Muslim forces. Bernard of Clairvaux, a fervent defender of the Templars, preached this crusade with passionate fervour, attracting knights from all over Europe, including King Louis VII of France and Emperor Conrad III of the Holy Roman Empire.

The Templars, already well established in the Holy Land, took an active part in this expedition. Their military discipline and knowledge of the terrain made them valuable allies for the crusading armies. During the battle of Dorylaeum in 1147, the Templars played a crucial role in protecting the retreat of Conrad's army, preventing a total defeat. Their courage and organization helped to limit losses and regain safer ground.

Conrad's army, weakened by the difficulties of the march through Anatolia and by the incessant attacks of the Turkish forces, indeed found indispensable support from the Templars. The latter, thanks to their rigorous training and their ability to maintain a defensive formation under pressure, managed to organize an orderly retreat, offering a lifeline to the imperial troops in disarray. This action demonstrated not only their bravery but also their ability to act decisively and coordinated in critical situations.

After this difficult retreat, the French army of Louis VII, accompanied by the Templars, arrived in turn in the Holy Land. The Templars, strong with their experience and their network of fortresses, played a key role in coordinating the efforts of the crusading forces. They provided not only a disciplined fighting force but also strategic advice based on their knowledge of the terrain and enemy tactics.

Despite their involvement and competence, the Second Crusade was marked by failures and disappointments. Internal conflicts among the crusader leaders, planning errors, and logistical difficulties weakened the effectiveness of the expedition. The attempt to take Damascus in 1148, in particular, ended in a resounding failure. The poorly planned attack and mistrust among the different Christian factions led to a hasty and humiliating retreat.

The Templars, although not responsible for the fatal strategic decisions, were also affected by this failure. Their military reputation, however, emerged relatively unscathed thanks to their performances on the battlefield and their ability to maintain order and discipline among the troops. Their role in protecting the Latin states of the East continued to strengthen, consolidating their position as indispensable defenders of Christianity in the Holy Land.

The end of the Second Crusade left a bitter taste and a feeling of disillusionment among the crusaders. Bernard of Clairvaux himself, who had preached with such fervour for this expedition, expressed his deep sadness and disappointment at the results. However, for the Templars, the experience gained during this crusade strengthened their commitment and resilience. Their ability to learn from strategic failures and maintain their discipline in adversity resulted in a continuous improvement of their tactics and command structures.

The impact of the Second Crusade on the order was also marked by an increased recognition of their importance. The Templars had proven that they were not only warriors but also competent strategists and organizers, capable of playing a central role in complex military enterprises. This recognition was manifested by additional donations of land and wealth from European nobles, further strengthening their influence and autonomy.

Furthermore, the crusade provided the Templars with the opportunity to strengthen their alliances with other military orders and local political factions. Their interaction with the Hospitallers evolved into a closer cooperation, albeit punctuated by rivalries. Together, they shared crucial information and coordinated their efforts to defend the Latin states against Muslim attacks. These alliances contributed to a more coherent and effective defence of the Holy Land.

The position of the Templars in medieval society also strengthened. Their crucial role during the Second Crusade and their exemplary behaviour on the battlefield helped to forge their image as devoted defenders of Christianity. This positive perception increased their prestige among laypeople and religious, increasing their ability to recruit new members and receive donations. The Templar castles, scattered across Europe and the Middle East, became centres of military and economic power, consolidating their role in the fabric of medieval society.

The end of the Second Crusade also marked a turning point in the crusaders' approach to war in the Holy Land. The Templars, learning from their experiences, adopted more defensive and pragmatic strategies. They strengthened their fortifications, improved their logistics, and developed espionage networks to better anticipate enemy movements. These strategic adjustments increased their effectiveness and resilience against the increasingly organized Muslim forces.

Despite the setbacks suffered during the Second Crusade, the order of the Templars emerged from this period stronger and more determined. Their active participation and unwavering dedication left a lasting imprint on the history of the crusades. They continued to play a central role in Christian military endeavours, their exploits and bravery becoming legendary. The Second Crusade, although a strategic failure, became a springboard for the order, solidifying their place as pillars of Christian defence in the Holy Land.

The Third Crusade.

The Third Crusade (1189-1192), triggered in response to the capture of Jerusalem by Saladin in 1187, saw the participation of iconic figures such as Richard the Lionheart of England, Philip Augustus of France, and Frederick Barbarossa of the Holy Roman Empire. The

Templars, at the forefront of the defence of the Latin states, played a decisive role in this campaign.

At the Battle of Acre, in 1189, the Templars demonstrated their worth by actively participating in the siege that lasted nearly two years. Their expertise in military engineering and their bravery in assaults were key elements in the capture of the city. Richard the Lionheart, impressed by their dedication and discipline, forged a close alliance with the Templars, relying on their knowledge of the terrain and their network of fortresses to conduct his campaigns.

The siege of Acre was one of the most crucial episodes of the crusade, and the participation of the Templars was decisive. They brought not only their military expertise but also essential logistical organization to support the crusader troops during this long and gruelling period. Their ability to build and maintain siege machines, as well as their aptitude to organize coordinated assaults, played a major role in the fall of the city into the hands of the crusaders in 1191.

After the capture of Acre, the Templars continued to play a central role in the military efforts of the crusade. Richard the Lionheart, renowned for his courage and tenacity, found in them trustworthy allies. Together, they undertook several expeditions aimed at weakening Muslim positions and recovering strategic territories. The Templars, with their network of fortresses, provided secure bases for military operations and served as essential supply points.

One of the notable battles of this crusade was that of Arsuf in September 1191. Here, the Templars, alongside the Hospitallers and Richard's troops, confronted Saladin's forces. The battle, intense and fierce, highlighted the bravery of the Templars who, under Richard's orders, charged the enemy lines with unwavering determination. Their intervention allowed to repel Saladin's forces and to achieve a decisive victory. This battle further cemented the alliance between Richard and the Templars, who became indispensable actors in the fight for the Holy Land.

The strategy of the Templars, focused on defence and securing pilgrimage routes, also proved crucial. Their network of fortresses, like those of Gaza, Safed and Tortosa, constituted impregnable bastions that protected the reclaimed territories and ensured a constant military presence. These fortresses served as shields against enemy incursions and as support points for the crusaders' offensive operations.

However, despite the victories and advances, the crusade did not manage to achieve its ultimate goal: the reconquest of Jerusalem. The negotiations with Saladin led to a truce, known as the Treaty of Jaffa, signed in 1192. This treaty allowed Christian pilgrims to freely visit the holy places, but Jerusalem remained under Muslim control. The Templars, while respecting this truce, continued to fortify their positions and prepare for possible future confrontations.

The outcome of the Third Crusade left mixed feelings among the crusaders. On one hand, they had secured strategic territories and established solid bases for the defence of the Latin states. On the other hand, the dream of retaking Jerusalem remained unfinished. The Templars, despite their disappointment, drew valuable lessons from this experience. They improved their fortifications, strengthened their alliances, and continued to develop their logistical and military networks.

The return of Richard the Lionheart to Europe did not weaken the ties between the Templars and the English crown. Richard, grateful for their support, granted them privileges and donations that further strengthened their position in Europe. The Templars, drawing on their experience in the Holy Land, also played an increased role in European affairs, offering their services as military and financial advisors to sovereigns and nobles.

The Third Crusade, although partially successful, demonstrated the strategic importance of the Templars in crusade efforts. Their ability to organize, defend, and lead complex military campaigns made them indispensable allies for any future expedition to the Holy Land. Their influence expanded, and their reputation as formidable knights and unwavering defenders of the Christian faith was strengthened.

The Fourth Crusade.

Although the Fourth Crusade (1202-1204) was marked by detours and diverted objectives, the Templars maintained their presence in the Holy Land, continuing to defend Christian territories and protect pilgrims. They did not directly participate in the sack of Constantinople, a tragedy that divided Christendom, but continued to focus their efforts on the defence of the Latin states of the East.

The diversion of the Fourth Crusade towards Constantinople was a consequence of complex circumstances and diversified interests, including the debts of the crusaders to the Venetians and Byzantine political intrigues. The Templars, although concerned with developments in Europe, remained focused on their main mission: the protection of pilgrims and territories under Christian control in the Holy Land. Their absence during the sack of Constantinople allowed them to maintain a certain moral distance from this controversial event, thus reinforcing their reputation as defenders of Christian ideals.

While the Crusaders were heading towards Constantinople, the Templars in the Holy Land were facing constant challenges from local Muslim forces. Their fortresses, scattered at strategic points, served as bastions against enemy incursions. They undertook fortification work and improved their defences, ensuring that their positions could withstand prolonged sieges. These efforts included not only solid constructions, but also supply and communication strategies to support extended defences.

Their commitment to protecting pilgrims remained at the heart of their mission. The pilgrimage routes, often dangerous, were secured by Templar patrols who escorted groups of travellers, ensuring their safe passage to the holy places. The Templars, with their network of outposts and garrisons, were able to offer refuges and supply points, minimizing the risks for the pilgrims.

Meanwhile, the Templars continued to play a crucial role in the political affairs of the Latin states of the East. Their influence extended beyond the battlefields, leading them to become advisors and mediators in local conflicts. Their relative impartiality and commitment to the Christian cause gave them a moral authority that was respected by the different factions. They participated in war councils and strategic decisions, bringing their experience and unique military perspective.

The Fourth Crusade, although far from its initial objectives, had repercussions on the Latin states of the East and the Templars. The sack of Constantinople in 1204 weakened the Byzantine Empire and redistributed power in the region, creating new political and military dynamics. The Templars had to adapt to these changes, strengthening their alliances and reevaluating their strategies to ensure the survival and stability of the remaining Christian territories.

The wealth and treasures brought back from Constantinople by the crusaders enriched some participants, but the Templars, who remained in the Holy Land, continued to finance their activities through donations and the income from their European possessions. Their banking network and rigorous management of resources allowed them to maintain a strong presence despite political upheavals.

As news of the sack of Constantinople spread, the Templars faced moral and spiritual challenges. They had to reconcile their sacred mission with the complex political and military realities of the time. The diversion of the crusade and the resulting violence highlighted the tensions between Christian ideals and the actions of the crusaders. The Templars, as a religious and military order, often found themselves navigating between these two poles, seeking to remain faithful to their original mission while adapting to the pragmatic demands of war and politics.

Their role as protectors of pilgrims and defenders of Latin states continued with renewed determination. The Templars invested in improving their military capabilities, adopting new siege technologies and perfecting their combat techniques. They continued to recruit knights devoted to their cause, integrating diverse skills to strengthen their order.

Despite the upheavals caused by the Fourth Crusade, the Templars remained a pillar of Christian defence in the Holy Land. Their resilience in the face of challenges, their commitment to their mission, and their ability to adapt to political and military changes allowed them to maintain their position and ensure the protection of pilgrims. The Templar fortresses, symbols of their power and dedication, remained bastions of security and faith in a region marked by instability and conflict.

The Fifth Crusade.

The Fifth Crusade (1217-1221), which aimed to capture Jerusalem by attacking Egypt, once again saw the active participation of the Templars. Under the command of the papal legate Pelagius and John of Brienne, king of Jerusalem, the Templars played a crucial role in the battles of Damietta. Their discipline and military experience allowed the crusaders to capture the city in 1219. However, internal dissensions and strategic errors led to the loss of Damietta in 1221, despite the heroic efforts of the Templars to maintain the position.

When the Crusaders decided to focus their efforts on Egypt, they hoped to strike a decisive blow against the Ayyubid Sultanate, thinking that the capture of this key territory would significantly weaken the Muslim forces and pave the way for the reconquest of Jerusalem. The Templars, with their experience from previous campaigns, were essential in the planning and execution of this bold strategy. Their reputation for expertise in military engineering and siege strategy placed them at the heart of operations.

The Templars brought with them a well-equipped fleet and a disciplined army. They played a crucial role in the maritime blockade of Damietta, cutting off supplies and isolating the city. Their ability to maintain a prolonged siege, despite difficult conditions, was decisive for the initial success of the crusade. The discipline and endurance of the Templars allowed them to overcome logistical challenges and enemy counterattacks.

In 1219, after months of rigorous siege, the crusaders managed to breach the defences of Damietta. The capture of the city was a moment of triumph, where the Templars demonstrated once again their worth on the battlefield. Their methodical organization and their ability to lead coordinated assaults were key factors in this victory. The fall of Damietta strengthened the position of the crusaders and gave them a strategic outpost for future operations in Egypt.

However, the crusade was quickly marked by internal divisions and strategic disagreements. The papal legate Pelagius, fervent and determined, came into conflict with other crusade leaders, including Jean de Brienne. The Templars, although accustomed to navigating the tumultuous waters of crusade politics, often found themselves torn between different factions. Their loyalty to the Church and their military mission pushed them to support Pelagius's efforts, but the dissensions weakened the effectiveness of the operations.

The major strategic error occurred when the crusaders decided to march towards Cairo, hoping to capitalize on their success in Damietta. However, this decision proved disastrous. The crusader forces, ill-prepared for the harsh conditions of the Nile Valley, quickly found themselves in trouble. The floods and the tenacious resistance of the Ayyubid forces, commanded by Sultan Al-Kamil, made progress impossible.

The Templars, despite their bravery and military expertise, could not compensate for the command errors and poor logistical planning. They fought heroically to protect the retreat of the crusaders and maintain a defensive line against the relentless attacks of the Muslim forces. Their discipline and ability to organize defences in the background helped to minimize losses, but the situation became increasingly desperate.

In 1221, the crusaders were forced to accept a truce and withdraw from Damietta, surrendering the city to the Ayyubid forces in exchange for the freedom of their captured troops. This capitulation, although necessary to save the lives of the crusaders, was a heavy blow to the crusade and a major strategic failure. The Templars, who had invested so much in this campaign, saw their efforts reduced to nothing by internal divisions and command errors.

Despite the defeat, the Templars drew important lessons from this experience. Their ability to maintain discipline and execute complex operations under adverse conditions was strengthened. They continued to improve their siege tactics and strengthen their fortifications in the Holy Land, anticipating future confrontations. Their unwavering commitment to the protection of pilgrims and Christian territories did not waver, despite setbacks.

The Sixth Crusade.

The Sixth Crusade (1228-1229), led by Emperor Frederick II, was unique in that it managed to recover Jerusalem without major combat, thanks to diplomatic negotiations with Sultan Al-Kamil. The Templars, although sceptical of Frederick's method, supported the crusade by providing a military presence and securing Christian positions once the agreements were concluded.

Emperor Frederick II, a man of great culture and strategic vision, undertook this crusade with a radically different approach from his predecessors. Known for his diplomatic skills as much as for his military talents, Frederick managed to enter into negotiations with Sultan Al-Kamil, ruler of Ayyubid Egypt. Al-Kamil, aware of potential threats from other fronts and eager to stabilize his borders, was open to an agreement.

Frederick II, accompanied by a crusader army partly made up of Templars, sailed towards the Holy Land with a clear objective but an unconventional method. The Templars, whose experience and presence in the Holy Land were invaluable, were initially suspicious. They were accustomed to methods of conquest by force and the fierce defence of their fortresses. However, their allegiance to the Christian cause and their pragmatism led them to support Frederick's efforts, even if the means employed differed from their expectations.

The negotiations between Frederick and Al-Kamil were long and complex, marked by exchanges of letters and diplomatic meetings. The Templars, although primarily warriors, understood the importance of these talks. They ensured the protection of areas under Christian control, guaranteeing that the crusading forces remained ready to act in case of a breakdown in negotiations.

The treaty of 1229, resulting from negotiations, was an unprecedented diplomatic success for a crusade. Al-Kamil agreed to cede Jerusalem, Bethlehem and Nazareth to the Christians, while retaining control of the sacred Muslim sites in the city. This restitution of Jerusalem, obtained without bloodshed, was a triumph for Frederick II and a surprise for the Christian world. The Templars, although surprised by the effectiveness of this diplomatic approach, recognized the importance of this strategic gain.

Once the agreement was signed, the Templars played a crucial role in securing Jerusalem. They took charge of fortifying the city's defences, repairing the walls and strengthening key positions. Their expertise in military engineering and garrison management quickly stabilized the situation, ensuring that Jerusalem would be defensible against any future attack.

The relationship between Frederick II and the Templars was complex. Although Frederick succeeded where so many others had failed, his unconventional method and his tensions with Pope Gregory IX created frictions. The Templars, faithful to the Church, sometimes found themselves in a delicate position, balancing their support for Frederick with their loyalty to the pontiff.

By securing Jerusalem, the Templars reaffirmed their role as protectors of the holy places. Their presence continued to symbolize the resilience and strength of Christianity in the Holy Land. Although the method of reclaiming Jerusalem was unusual, the results were tangible and strategically significant. The Templars, adapting their skills to this new reality, played an indispensable role in consolidating the gains obtained through diplomacy.

The agreement of 1229 did not signify the end of challenges for Christians in the Holy Land. Tensions remained, and fragile alliances could break at any moment. The Templars, aware of these fragilities, continued to strengthen their positions and prepare defences in anticipation of future conflicts. Their ability to foresee and prepare for difficult eventualities made them a stabilizing force in a region constantly threatened by political and military upheavals.

The Seventh Crusade.

The Seventh Crusade (1248-1254), led by King Louis IX of France, was an ambitious endeavour aimed at weakening Muslim forces by attacking Egypt, considered the nerve centre of Ayyubid power. The Templars, always at the forefront of crusading efforts, played a crucial role in this campaign, providing not only a disciplined military force but also strategic advice based on their extensive experience of wars in the Holy Land.

King Louis IX, driven by deep faith and unwavering determination, mobilized an imposing army for this crusade. In 1248, he left France with a well-equipped fleet and a contingent of knights, ready to face the challenges that awaited him in Egypt. The Templars, with their established reputation as seasoned fighters and competent strategists, were integrated into the main forces, offering their invaluable expertise to navigate difficult terrains and complex battles.

The landing in Egypt marked the beginning of a series of intense military manoeuvres. In June 1249, after a coordinated offensive, the crusader forces managed to capture Damietta, marking an important initial victory. This capture, although significant, was only the beginning of the challenges the crusaders were going to face.

After the capture of Damietta, Louis IX and his advisors, including the Templars, decided to march towards Cairo, hoping to deal a decisive blow to the Muslim forces. However, this decision proved to be perilous. The Templars, although competent in military strategy, could not compensate for the logistical difficulties and unfavourable environmental conditions.

The decisive battle took place near the city of Mansoura in 1250. The Templars, alongside the Knights of Saint John and the French royal troops, engaged the forces of Emir Fakhr al-Din. The battle was fierce and marked by relentless fighting. The Templars, known for their discipline and bravery, resisted valiantly, but the adverse conditions and the skilled tactics of the Muslim forces overcame the crusader army. Confusion and disorganization took over, leading to a severe defeat for the crusaders.

Louis IX, along with several nobles and knights, was captured during this battle. The Templars, although decimated, continued to fight to protect their king and their companions. The capture of Louis IX was a hard blow for the crusaders, but subsequent negotiations ensured his release in exchange for a massive ransom and the return of Damietta to the Muslim forces. The Templars played a crucial role in these negotiations, using their influence and network to facilitate discussions and ensure the safety of the prisoners.

Despite military setbacks, the Templars emerged from the Seventh Crusade with their reputation intact, if not strengthened. Their ability to withstand under extreme conditions and their unwavering dedication to the Christian cause were recognized by Louis IX and his advisors.

The crusade itself, although considered a military failure, demonstrated the ongoing importance of the Templars in the crusading efforts. Their role was not limited to battles; they were also diplomats, negotiators, and strategists, navigating the political and military complexities of the region.

Upon returning to Europe, Louis IX, deeply marked by the events, undertook to reform and strengthen the military and religious institutions, often drawing inspiration from Templar practices. The Templars, benefiting from this royal support, continued to play a central role in preparations for future crusades, by training new knights and consolidating their resources.

The Eighth Crusade.

The Eighth Crusade (1270), initiated by King Louis IX of France, was an endeavour marked by unforeseen circumstances and insurmountable challenges. Louis IX, known for his piety and dedication to the Christian cause, undertook this crusade in the hope of strengthening Christian positions in the Holy Land. The Templars, faithful to their mission of defending Christianity, fully committed to this expedition, bringing their military expertise and invaluable experience.

Louis IX's decision to launch the Eighth Crusade was motivated by a renewed desire to correct the failures of previous crusades and to respond to Rome's constant call for the protection of holy places. Louis IX, accompanied by his army and the Templars, set off for Tunis in 1270, with the initial intention of securing the region before progressing to Jerusalem. Tunis, under the rule of the Hafsid Sultanate, was seen as a strategic step to weaken Muslim forces and establish an advanced base for future operations in the Holy Land.

However, upon their arrival in Tunis, the crusaders were confronted with unexpected difficulties. An epidemic of dysentery and scurvy spread rapidly among the troops, severely weakening the soldiers. The Templars, despite their rigorous training, were not spared from the disease. Their discipline and organization allowed them to maintain a semblance of order and continue operations, but the human losses were heavy.

The situation became even more critical when Louis IX himself succumbed to illness on August 25, 1270. The king's death was a terrible blow to the crusade, plunging the crusaders into disarray and uncertainty. The Templars, as guardians of order and stability, played a key role in reorganizing the forces and attempting to maintain troop morale. Their leadership and resilience were essential to prevent a total collapse.

Charles of Anjou, brother of Louis IX, took command of the crusading army after the king's death. Under his leadership, the crusaders attempted to pursue the campaign's objectives. The Templars, although affected by losses and diseases, continued to defend Christian positions with courage and determination. They participated in negotiations with the Sultan of Tunis, which resulted in a favourable treaty allowing the crusaders to withdraw honourably while obtaining economic and religious concessions.

The Eighth Crusade, although marked by tragedy and difficulties, once again revealed the Templars' ability to adapt and persevere. The agreements obtained with the Sultan of Tunis, although far from the initial objectives, allowed to secure advantages for the Christians and to avoid a total defeat. The return of the crusaders to Europe marked the end of the Eighth Crusade, but the impact of this expedition was felt long after.

The Defence of the Holy Land.

Throughout the Crusades, the Templars were the staunch defenders of the Latin states of the East. They built and maintained strategic fortresses, such as the Krak des Chevaliers and the fortress of Safed, which became impregnable bastions. These fortresses, erected with advanced engineering, served as essential defence points against Muslim incursions.

The Templars, through their constant presence and unwavering commitment, embodied the spirit of the crusade. They were the protectors of pilgrims, the guardians of roads, and the champions of the Christian faith. Their participation in the crusades was not only military, but also spiritual, each battle being perceived as a personal crusade against the forces of evil.

Conclusion.

The participation of the Templars in the crusades was an epic of courage, sacrifice, and faith. They stood as living ramparts, defending the holy places with unwavering determination. Through victories and defeats, their dedication remained a constant, making them the sacred guardians of Christianity in the Holy Land. Their legacy, forged in the fire of the crusades, continues to resonate through the ages, symbolizing the marriage of faith and bravery.

At the Heart of the Battle: The Greatest Battles and Sieges of the Templars.

In the clash of swords and the rolling of war drums, the Templar knights distinguished themselves with their bravery and devotion during the great battles and sieges that marked the history of the Crusades. Their red cross, a symbol of their sacred commitment, shone on the battlefields, inspiring courage and terror. From the capture of Jerusalem to the last resistances in the Holy Land, the Templars were the relentless defenders of Christianity, forging their legend through epic battles and heroic sieges.

The Capture of Jerusalem (1099).

The capture of Jerusalem in 1099. Under the banner of the first crusade, European knights, after a long and gruelling siege, managed to penetrate the Holy City. The fall of Jerusalem was marked by intense religious fervour and unprecedented violence. The city, a sanctuary for several religions, became the scene of a massacre where the crusaders, drunk with victory and devotion, purged Jerusalem of its Muslim and Jewish occupants.

Launched by Pope Urban II in 1095 at the Council of Clermont, the First Crusade aimed to liberate Jerusalem and other holy sites from Muslim hands. The Pope's call resonated deeply in European hearts, mobilizing thousands of knights, peasants, and pilgrims united by an unprecedented religious zeal. These crusaders undertook a perilous journey across Europe and Asia Minor, facing numerous natural and human obstacles. After months of marching and sporadic fighting, they finally reached the imposing walls of Jerusalem in June 1099.

The siege of Jerusalem was one of the most arduous and symbolic of the entire crusade campaign. The crusaders, exhausted by the long journey and previous battles, found themselves facing a fortified and well-defended city. The crusader army was made up of contingents from various regions of Europe, each with its own leaders and tactics. Despite these diversities, they shared a common determination: the conviction that God had chosen them for this sacred mission.

Under the command of leaders such as Godefroy de Bouillon, Raymond IV of Toulouse, and Tancred of Hauteville, the crusaders undertook repeated assaults against the walls of Jerusalem. The initial efforts were unsuccessful, with the Fatimid defence being particularly tenacious. The crusaders had to resort to ingenious military engineering, building siege towers and battering rams to try to break the defences. The stifling heat of the summer, the lack of water and food made the situation almost unbearable.

The desperate situation of the Crusaders was suddenly transformed by what they perceived as a divine miracle. According to the accounts, a religious procession around the city walls, inspired by a spiritual vision, gave the Crusaders renewed fervour. They launched a final assault with redoubled energy. On July 15, 1099, after a siege of several weeks, the Crusaders managed to penetrate the city through the Saint Stephen's gate. That day, the capture of Jerusalem became a bloody reality.

The fall of Jerusalem was marked by extreme violence. The crusaders, intoxicated by their victory and religious devotion, indulged in indiscriminate slaughter. The chronicles of the time, although biased and often exaggerated, describe scenes of carnage where Muslims and Jews were killed by the thousands. The city streets were turned into rivers of blood, and religious sanctuaries, desecrated by the attackers, were purged of their occupants. The Basilica of the Holy Sepulchre, a symbol of Christianity, was cleaned and consecrated anew by the victorious crusaders.

This capture of Jerusalem, although tragic in its brutality, marked a decisive turning point in the history of the Crusades. It reinforced the crusaders' belief that their mission was supported by divine will. Godefroy de Bouillon, one of the leaders of the crusade, refused the title of king, preferring that of "Protector of the Holy Sepulchre", thus emphasizing the sacred nature of their conquest.

The capture of Jerusalem also had lasting consequences on the geopolitics of the region. It marked the beginning of the Latin States of the East, Christian political entities established on formerly Muslim lands. These new states, including the Kingdom of Jerusalem, became Christian bastions in the Holy Land, requiring constant defence against Muslim counterattacks. It was in this context of a constant need for protection that the idea of an order of knights dedicated to the defence of pilgrims and holy places began to germinate, leading to the creation of the Templars about twenty years later.

The Battle of Montgisard (1177).

One of the most resounding victories of the Templars took place during the Battle of Montgisard, on November 25, 1177. Saladin, the powerful Ayyubid sultan, was launching a major offensive against the Crusader kingdoms. Baldwin IV, the leper king of Jerusalem, accompanied by a small force including the Templar knights, found himself facing Saladin's superior army. Against all odds, the Crusaders led a desperate charge, with the Templars at the forefront, inflicting a decisive defeat on Saladin. The victory of Montgisard became a symbol of the courage and faith of the Templars, capable of overturning much more powerful forces through their bravery and determination.

The year 1177 was a period of extreme tension for the Latin states of Jerusalem. Saladin, having consolidated his power in Egypt and Syria, sought to destroy the Christian enclaves and permanently secure the region under his control. In November, he gathered a considerable army and marched north, expecting an easy victory against the weakened Christian forces. News of Saladin's approach reached Baldwin IV, an admirable king despite his youth and illness. At only 16 years old, Baldwin IV suffered from leprosy, but this did not weaken his determination or courage.

Baldwin IV, aware of the imminent threat, gathered a small force composed of knights, soldiers from various factions and, crucially, the Templars, led by their grand master. The Templars, with their discipline and experience, formed the backbone of this reduced army. The king and his troops quickly left Jerusalem to intercept Saladin before he could besiege the city or take key positions.

The encounter between the two armies took place near Montgisard, a place that quickly became synonymous with military miracle. Faced with a much larger and better equipped Ayyubid army, the Crusaders found themselves in an apparently desperate situation. But Baldwin IV, carrying a relic of the True Cross, galvanized his men, urging them to fight with renewed faith. The Templars, always at the forefront, prepared for a decisive charge.

The battle began under unlikely auspices. Saladin, confident in his numerical and strategic superiority, was surprised by the fury of the Christian attack. The Crusaders, led by the Templars, launched a bold frontal charge that broke the Muslim lines. The discipline and tight formation of the Templars allowed them to maintain the initial impact and cause considerable chaos among Saladin's troops. The terrain, narrow and favourable to tight defences, also played in favour of the Crusaders.

The Battle of Montgisard was characterized by an intensity and brutality that deeply marked the participants from both sides. The Templars demonstrated an uncommon resilience and determination. Their ability to maintain cohesion and inflict severe losses despite their numerical inferiority proved decisive. Saladin, for the first time in his career, was forced to retreat in a disorganized manner, leaving behind a large part of his army and equipment.

The accounts of the battle tell how Saladin, distraught, escaped with only a handful of bodyguards, his confidence in an easy victory transformed into a humiliating defeat. The Muslim losses were heavy, and Saladin's hasty retreat allowed the crusaders to achieve a victory not only military but also moral. The news of the victory at Montgisard spread quickly, boosting the morale of the crusaders and inspiring a new wave of devotion and determination to defend the Christian territories.

The battle of Montgisard had profound repercussions on the dynamics of the Crusades. It demonstrated that even a numerically inferior army could inflict a significant defeat on a dominant force, thanks to faith, determination, and strategy. The Templars, emerging from this battle with increased prestige, were celebrated for their crucial role in the victory. Their bravery and skill as a shock force became legendary, reinforcing their reputation as formidable and devoted warriors.

Baldwin IV, despite his illness, became a symbolic hero of Christian resistance, his leadership during the battle being hailed as exemplary. The victory at Montgisard delayed Saladin's ambitions to dominate the Latin states and allowed the Crusaders to gain precious time to strengthen their defences and prepare for future campaigns. This victory, although not eliminating the threat posed by Saladin, demonstrated that determination and faith could overcome seemingly insurmountable obstacles.

The Siege of Acre (1189-1191).

The siege of Acre was one of the longest and bloodiest battles of the Crusades. Begun in 1189, this siege lasted nearly two years and became a focal point of the Third Crusade. Acre, a strategic fortified city on the Mediterranean coast, was held by Saladin's Muslim forces. The Templars, with their expertise in military engineering and their inflexible discipline, played a crucial role in the repeated assaults and defences.

The Crusaders, under the command of Guy de Lusignan, King of Jerusalem, began the siege in August 1189. From the outset, they faced fierce resistance from the Muslim garrison of Acre, supported by regular reinforcements from Saladin. The Templars, known for their discipline and ability to conduct prolonged sieges, found themselves at the heart of efforts to break the city's defences. They built siege machines, towers and battering rams, and organized coordinated assaults against the imposing walls of Acre.

The conditions of the siege were terrible. Famine and disease ravaged the ranks of the crusaders, weakening their ability to maintain an effective blockade. The Templars, although better organized and prepared than many of their allies, were not spared from these plagues. Despite this, their discipline and resilience allowed them to maintain constant pressure on the Muslim defenders. The Templars, alongside other military orders like the Hospitallers, played a crucial role in consolidating positions and protecting the crusader camps against Saladin's counterattacks.

The arrival of Richard the Lionheart of England and Philip Augustus of France in 1191 brought a renewal of energy and resources to the crusading forces. Richard, in particular, demonstrated charismatic and determined leadership. The Templars, admiring his military skills, found in him a powerful ally. Richard the Lionheart, aware of the value of the Templars, relied on their expertise to plan and execute decisive assaults against the fortifications of Acre.

The clashes around the city reached an unprecedented level of violence. The Templars, often on the front line, suffered heavy losses but continued to fight with unwavering determination. The street fights, once the walls were partially broken, were particularly brutal. The crusaders had to conquer each house, each street, facing desperate resistance from the Muslim defenders. The Templars, with their rigorous training and esprit de corps, played a key role in these close-quarters battles.

In parallel, the Templars also took part in trench warfare and undermining operations aimed at weakening the foundations of the walls. Their advanced knowledge in military engineering allowed them to carry out complex undermining operations, digging tunnels under the walls to cause collapses. These efforts, although dangerous and often deadly, were essential in breaching the defences of Acre.

The siege of Acre was not limited to land battles. As the city was a port, naval battles played a crucial role. The crusader fleets, reinforced by Genoese and Venetian ships, blocked the city's maritime supplies. The Templars, with their own ships and experienced sailors, significantly contributed to this blockade. They participated in several naval battles, ensuring that Saladin's reinforcements and supplies could not reach the besieged city.

After nearly two years of relentless fighting, the situation in Acre became critical for the Muslim defenders. The morale of Saladin's troops was collapsing, while the crusaders, galvanized by the arrival of new reinforcements and the determination of their leaders, intensified their assaults. In July 1191, the garrison of Acre, exhausted and short of resources, finally surrendered to the crusaders. The capture of Acre, although costly in human lives, marked a decisive turning point in the Third Crusade.

The victory at Acre allowed for the reestablishment of a strong Christian presence in the Holy Land. The Templars, having played a central role in this success, saw their prestige and influence strengthened. The capture of Acre provided the crusaders with a strategic base for future military operations and became a crucial centre for commercial and military activities in the region. The Templars, in recognition of their efforts and sacrifice, received positions and privileges in the conquered city.

For Richard the Lionheart, the victory at Acre reinforced his reputation as a great military leader. His alliance with the Templars became even stronger, each respecting the skills and courage of the other. This cooperation between Richard and the Templars became a model of effective collaboration between royal forces and religious military orders, unifying efforts for common goals.

The Battle of Hattin (1187).

The Battle of Hattin was a devastating defeat for the Latin States of the East and a tragic turning point in the history of the Templars. On July 4, 1187, the Crusader forces, weakened by thirst and heat, found themselves surrounded by Saladin's army near the Horns of Hattin, two volcanic hills located in Galilee. Despite their bravery, the Crusaders, including many Templars, were crushed by Saladin's superior forces.

Tensions between Christian and Muslim forces were at their peak during the summer of 1187. Saladin, determined to reconquer Jerusalem and drive the Crusaders out of the Holy Land, assembled a massive army. On the other side, Guy de Lusignan, King of Jerusalem, assembled an impressive force composed of knights and soldiers from various Latin states, including the formidable Templars. Confident in their cause and in the protection of the True Cross, a sacred relic carried by the Crusaders, they marched to confront Saladin.

However, the strategic decisions that followed proved to be fatal. Guy de Lusignan, influenced by advisors and the need to respond to Saladin's provocations, chose to leave the safety of Sephoria to march towards the lake of Tiberias. This movement, although aimed at lifting the siege of Tiberias, exposed the crusading forces to thirst and the intense heat of the desert. The Templars, despite their discipline and experience, could not escape the terrible conditions and the ambushes of the Muslim army.

The march quickly turned into an unbearable ordeal. Water became scarce, and the exhausted soldiers were continually harassed by the rapid and effective attacks of Saladin's cavalry. By the time the crusaders reached the Horns of Hattin, they were already considerably weakened. Saladin, a brilliant strategist, took advantage of their vulnerability to completely encircle them. As night fell, the crusaders found themselves trapped, with no hope of reinforcements or resupply.

On the morning of July 4th, the battle truly began. The crusaders, desperately trying to break through enemy lines, were confronted with a rain of arrows and relentless charges from Saladin's cavalry. The Templars, alongside the Hospitallers, formed the heart of the crusader resistance. Their bravery and discipline were exemplary, but faced with the numerical and tactical superiority of the enemy, they could not maintain their positions. Saladin's assaults, methodically planned, wreaked havoc among the crusader ranks.

The most poignant symbol of this defeat was the capture of the True Cross. This sacred relic, carried into battle by the crusaders, was a powerful symbol of their faith and mission. Its capture by the Muslim forces represented not only a material loss but also a devastating spiritual blow to the crusaders. The cross, which had inspired so many victorious battles, became a war trophy for Saladin.

Among the captives was Gérard de Ridefort, the Grand Master of the Templars. Saladin, aware of the threat posed by the Templars, ordered the execution of most of the captured Templar knights. They were seen as the most formidable and uncompromising enemies of Islam, their devotion and military skill being recognized and feared. Gérard de Ridefort, however, escaped this execution, a fate that would mark the future events of the order.

The defeat at Hattin paved the way for Saladin's reconquest of Jerusalem. News of the defeat spread quickly, sowing despair among the Christian populations of the Latin states. Fortresses and cities, once bastions of Christianity, fell one after the other in the face of the relentless advance of Muslim forces. Jerusalem, the ultimate symbol of Christian faith, capitulated in October 1187, marking the end of an era of Crusader domination in the Holy Land.

For the Templars, the Battle of Hattin was a tragic turning point. Their reputation as invincible warriors took a hit, but their devotion and mission remained intact. They withdrew to reorganize their forces, determined to resume the fight for Jerusalem and the holy places. Their sacrifice at Hattin, although painful, reinforced their legend as martyrs of the Christian faith, ready to sacrifice everything for their sacred mission.

The Siege of Safed (1266).

The Safed Castle, one of the main Templar fortresses in Galilee, was the scene of an epic siege in 1266. The Mamluk forces, under the direction of Sultan Baybars, launched a massive attack against this imposing fortress. The Templars, well entrenched and determined, valiantly resisted. However, after a long and arduous siege, marked by repeated assaults and internal betrayals, Safed fell into the hands of the Mamluks.

The Safed Castle, perched on a strategic hill overlooking the region, represented a key position for the Templars and Crusaders in Galilee. Built with advanced engineering and fortified to withstand the most violent assaults, Safed was a symbol of Christian power in the region. Its fall would have profound implications not only for the Templars but for the entire Christian presence in the Holy Land.

Baybars, the formidable Mamluk sultan, known for his military skills and his determination to eradicate the Crusader presence in the Holy Land, understood the strategic importance of Safed. In 1266, he assembled a massive army and marched on the fortress. The Mamluks, equipped with sophisticated siege machines and well-trained forces, began to besiege the castle.

The Templars, under the direction of their local commander, prepared for a fierce defence. Aware of the importance of Safed, they reinforced the walls, stocked up on provisions, and armed every man capable of carrying a weapon. Days and weeks passed, and the Mamluks intensified their assaults. The catapults launched flaming projectiles, and the battering rams attempted to break down the fortified doors.

The defence of Safed became an example of resilience and bravery. The Templars, despite their numerical inferiority, repelled the assaults with fierce determination. Each Mamluk attack met with fierce resistance, and losses accumulated on both sides. The Templars, experts in defensive tactics, used the fortress structures to their advantage, inflicting severe losses on the attackers.

However, the siege dragged on, and conditions inside the fortress became increasingly precarious. Food and water reserves began to run out, and physical and moral fatigue set in among the defenders. The Mamluks, under the constant pressure of Baybars, did not loosen their grip. They built tunnels to try to undermine the walls, and night attacks became commonplace to weaken the defenders' vigilance.

The situation became even more desperate when acts of internal betrayal were revealed. Spies or traitors within the walls of Safed provided crucial information to the attackers, allowing the Mamluks to target weak points in the defences. These betrayals undermined the morale of the Templars and made the task of defence even more difficult.

Finally, after months of relentless siege, the walls of Safed gave way under the continuous assaults. The Mamluks penetrated the fortress, and a bloody battle ensued in the courtyards and halls of the castle. The

Templars, refusing to surrender, fought until their last breath. Their bravery and determination, even in the face of certain death, were exemplary. The defenders were massacred, and Safed castle fell into the hands of the Mamluks.

The fall of Safed was a major strategic loss for the Templars and the Crusaders. It demonstrated the tenacity and sacrifice of the Templar knights, who, despite their fierce resistance, could not prevent the fortress from falling. Their bravery in the face of certain death became a legend, symbolizing their devotion to the last breath. The loss of Safed marked a critical stage in the collapse of Christian positions in the Holy Land and signalled the irreversible rise of the Mamluk forces.

Baybars, consolidating his victory, ordered the repair and strengthening of the fortifications of Safed, thus ensuring Mamluk control over this strategic position. The tales of the Templars' heroic defence at Safed spread quickly, inspiring both admiration and sadness among Western Christians. Their sacrifice symbolized the desperate struggle of the Crusaders to maintain their presence in the Holy Land in the face of increasingly dominant forces.

The Battle of La Forbie (1244).

The Battle of La Forbie, also known as the Battle of Harbiyah, in 1244, was one of the most disastrous battles for the Templars. A coalition of crusaders, including the Templars, the Hospitallers, and the Teutonic Knights, faced a combined force of Khwarezmians and Mamluks near Gaza. The crusaders, despite their bravery, were outmatched by the ferocity and strategy of their opponents.

In 1244, the Latin states of the Holy Land were in a precarious situation. Internal rivalries and constant threats from the surrounding Muslim powers made the survival of the Crusaders more difficult each day. The arrival of the Khwarezmians, nomadic warriors driven out by the Mongols, added a new threat. These Khwarezmians, wild and formidable, allied themselves with the Mamluks of Egypt, forming a formidable force that directly threatened Christian possessions.

The Christian coalition, composed of the Templars, the Hospitallers, the Teutonic Knights, and local forces, prepared to face this new threat. The Crusader command was aware that the upcoming battle would be decisive for the survival of their territories. The Templars, with their reputation for discipline and bravery, took a central place in the preparations. They knew that their role would be crucial in the effort to repel the invader.

On October 17, 1244, the two armies met near La Forbie, not far from Gaza. From the start, it became evident that the Muslim forces had the advantage in strategy and terrain. The Khwarezmians, with their mobility and harassment tactics, managed to disrupt the Crusader ranks. The Mamluks, competently led, launched coordinated attacks that exploited the weaknesses of the Christian positions.

The Templars, true to their reputation, fought with remarkable bravery and determination. They formed the heart of the resistance, holding their lines despite the ferocity of enemy assaults. Their banners flew high over the battlefield, symbolizing the unwavering commitment of the crusaders to defend their lands. However, the numerical superiority and superior strategy of the enemy forces began to tip the balance.

The Khwarezmians, using their knowledge of the terrain and their mobility, led devastating flank attacks. The crusader knights, although well-trained and disciplined, found themselves overwhelmed from all sides. The Mamluks, for their part, led frontal charges that broke the Christian defences. The Templars, caught between the two forces, fought desperately to maintain their positions.

The losses among the crusaders were catastrophic. The majority of the Templar knights present on the battlefield were killed or captured. The Hospitallers and the Teutonic Knights suffered similar losses. The battle turned into a massacre, with the crusaders fighting to the end but unable to repel the relentless waves of enemy attacks. The discipline of the Templars and their courage could not compensate for their numerical inferiority and the tactical superiority of their opponents.

The defeat at La Forbie had devastating consequences for the Christian forces in the Holy Land. It marked a turning point in the struggle against the rising Muslim powers. The losses in men and material severely weakened the military capabilities of the Crusaders. The capture of many experienced knights, including Templars, dealt a hard blow to the organization and morale of the Christian defenders.

This defeat weakened the position of the Latin States and opened the way for new advances by Muslim forces. The victorious Khwarezmians and Mamluks were able to exploit this victory to strengthen their grip on the region. The defeat at La Forbie became a symbol of the increasing difficulties faced by the Crusaders. It underscored the need for better coordination and strengthening of defences against increasingly powerful and organized enemies.

For the Templars, the battle of La Forbie was a bitter but crucial lesson. Their bravery and sacrifice were not forgotten, but they had to reorganize and prepare for new trials. The loss of so many experienced knights was a hard blow, but the order continued to recruit and train new members to carry on their mission. Their determination to defend the Holy Land and protect the pilgrims remained intact, even in the face of ever greater adversities.

The Defence of Acre (1291).

The Siege of Acre in 1291 was the final battle for the Templars in the Holy Land. Acre, the last bastion of the Crusaders, was besieged by the Mamluk forces led by Sultan al-Ashraf Khalil. The Templars, along with the Hospitallers and other Christian defenders, led a desperate and heroic defence.

Acre, capital of the Kingdom of Jerusalem since the loss of the holy city in 1187, represented the last bastion of the Latin states in the East. The city, fortified and strategically located on the Mediterranean coast, was an essential gateway for supplies and reinforcements from Europe. The Templars owned an imposing fortress there, a true bastion of their military and spiritual power. The fall of Acre would mean not only the end of a strategic position but also the symbolic collapse of Christian presence in the Holy Land.

In April 1291, the Mamluk forces, under the command of Sultan al-Ashraf Khalil, began their siege of the city. The Mamluk army, tens of thousands strong and equipped with powerful siege machines, launched a series of sustained attacks against the walls of Acre. The Christian defenders, including Templars, Hospitallers, and soldiers from various European factions, were determined to resist to the end.

The early days of the siege were marked by intense fighting and relentless assaults. The Mamluk war machines, notably the trebuchets, relentlessly bombarded the walls and towers of Acre, causing considerable destruction. The Templars, renowned for their discipline and bravery, held the most vulnerable points of the fortifications, repelling the attackers with fierce tenacity. The Grand Master of the Templars, Guillaume de Beaujeu, personally took part in the defence, leading his men with exemplary courage.

Despite the heroic efforts of the defenders, the walls of Acre began to give way under the constant pressure of the Mamluk assaults. Breaches appeared, and each day the fighting moved closer and closer to the heart of the city. The Templars, knowing the importance of every foot of ground, led desperate counterattacks to push the enemy out of the breaches, but the Mamluk forces were too numerous and too well organized.

On May 18, 1291, after nearly a month of siege, the Mamluks launched a massive attack that definitively broke the defences of Acre. Guillaume de Beaujeu, severely injured in the fighting, continued to lead his men until his injuries rendered him unable to continue. His last act of bravery and leadership inspired the Templars and other defenders to continue the fight, but the situation had become desperate.

In the streets of Acre, the fighting continued with unparalleled ferocity. The Templars, alongside the Hospitallers and armed citizens, fought house by house, street by street, refusing to yield despite the increasingly slim chances of survival. Accounts from the time describe scenes of carnage and despair, where each defender knew that the fall of the city would mean not only the end of their mission but also almost certain death.

Finally, the Christian defences completely collapsed. The Mamluk forces, penetrating the city, began to massacre the inhabitants and remaining defenders. Some Templars and Hospitallers managed to take refuge in the Templar fortress, hoping to hold out for a little longer. However, without hope of reinforcements and facing the inexorable enemy advance, even this last bastion could not resist indefinitely.

On May 28, the Templar fortress, the last refuge of the defenders of Acre, was finally taken. The surviving Templars were captured or killed, marking the end of the order in the Holy Land. Guillaume de Beaujeu, honoured by his brothers for his sacrifice and courage, symbolized the determination and dedication of the order in the face of overwhelming forces.

The fall of Acre on May 18, 1291 marked the end of the Crusader presence in the Holy Land. The Templars, retreating to Cyprus, were forced to reassess their role and mission. This defeat, although devastating, did not end the order, but it marked the end of an era of crusades. The heroism and sacrifice of the defenders of Acre became legends, inspiring future generations with their devotion and bravery.

The battle for Acre remains a poignant symbol of the Templars and Crusaders' relentless struggle to defend the Holy Land. Their desperate resistance and willingness to fight to the last man testify to their unwavering commitment to their cause and faith. The end of the Crusader presence in the Holy Land, although tragic, marked the beginning of a new phase for the Templars, who would continue to influence history and legend for centuries to come.

Conclusion.

The great battles and sieges in which the Templars participated were as many heroic and tragic chapters in the history of the Crusades. Their bravery, discipline, and devotion placed them at the heart of the most decisive and gruelling battles. From the capture of Jerusalem to the desperate defence of Acre, the Templars embodied the spirit of the Crusade, ready to sacrifice their lives for the Christian faith. Their legacy, forged in the fire and blood of battles, remains an eternal symbol of courage and sacrifice in the service of faith.

Strategic Role of the Templar Fortresses.

Under the azure sky of the Holy Land, the fortresses of the Templars rose like bastions of faith and resistance, marking the landscape with their imposing silhouette. These monumental structures, true masterpieces of military architecture, played a crucial role in the defence of the Latin States of the East. Designed to withstand the fiercest assaults and to shelter the defenders of Christendom, the Templar fortresses were symbols of the determination and ingenuity of the Knights Templar.

The Architecture of the Templar Fortresses.

The Templar fortresses were feats of engineering and design, built to maximize defence and resilience. Their construction took into account the technological advances of the time and lessons learned from previous battles. Each fortress was a combination of thick walls, massive towers, deep moats, and complex defence systems, created to withstand prolonged sieges.

The walls, often reinforced by several layers of stone, could reach impressive thicknesses, making their destruction by siege engines difficult. The watchtowers, placed at regular intervals along the ramparts, allowed for constant surveillance of the surroundings. The arrow slits and murder holes, narrow gaps in the walls, allowed the defenders to shoot at the attackers while remaining protected.

The fortresses were also equipped with sophisticated supply and storage systems, including cisterns for water and warehouses for food and ammunition. These provisions allowed the Templars to withstand prolonged sieges, often lasting several months, or even years. The internal infrastructures included housing, chapels, and workshops, making the fortresses self-sufficient microcosms.

The Krak of the Knights.

Among the most emblematic Templar fortresses is the Krak des Chevaliers, in Syria. Built on a strategic promontory, the Krak des Chevaliers is a perfect example of Templar military architecture. Its massive walls and imposing towers made it a virtually impregnable fortress. Designed to house a large garrison, it could accommodate several thousand knights and soldiers.

The Krak des Chevaliers controlled a crucial route between Homs and the Mediterranean Sea, serving as a passage point and protection for convoys and pilgrims. Its elevated position offered a panoramic view of the surroundings, allowing to detect enemy movements miles around. The Templars used this fortress not only as a defensive bastion, but also as a base of operations to launch raids and expeditions against the surrounding Muslim forces.

The Castle of Safed.

The Safed Castle, in Galilee, was another strategic fortress of the Templars. Erected on a hill overlooking the region, this fortress was essential for the defence of the north of the Kingdom of Jerusalem. Safed served as a checkpoint on the roads connecting Acre to Damascus, ensuring the security of communication and supply routes.

The fortress of Safed was surrounded by sturdy walls and watchtowers, equipped to withstand the most violent assaults. Despite its defences, it fell in 1266 into the hands of the Mamluks, after a fierce siege. The resistance of the Templars at Safed remains a testament to their bravery and unwavering commitment to defend their bastions to the last man.

The Fortress of Château Pèlerin.

Château Pèlerin, also known as Athlit, was a coastal fortress built by the Templars near Haifa. Located on a rocky peninsula jutting out into the Mediterranean Sea, Château Pèlerin was an impregnable stronghold, protected by the sea on three sides and by massive walls on the fourth.

Château Pèlerin served as a naval base and a starting point for the maritime expeditions of the Templars. It ensured the protection of ports and sea routes, facilitating the supply and reinforcement of garrisons in the Holy Land. Its strategic position made it an essential logistics centre for the crusades. The fortress also played a role as a refuge for pilgrims, offering a safe sanctuary on their route to Jerusalem.

The Role of Fortresses in Battles and Sieges.

The Templar fortresses were strategic pivots in battles and sieges. Their role exceeded that of simple defensive bastions; they were command and coordination centres, where battle plans were drawn up and forces were mobilized.

During sieges, the Templar fortresses served as refuges for civilian populations and fighters. Their ability to withstand prolonged assaults allowed for time to be gained, to attract enemy forces and to weaken them through attrition. The Templar garrisons, well-trained and disciplined, used active defence tactics, launching sorties to harass the besiegers and sabotage their siege engines.

Fortresses as Symbols of Power and Faith.

Beyond their military role, the Templar fortresses were symbols of power and faith. They represented the tangible presence of the Templar Order in the Holy Land, embodying their sacred mission to defend Christianity. The chapels within the fortresses were places of prayer and reflection, reminding the knights of their spiritual commitment.

The fortresses were also community centres, where knights and lay brothers lived, worked, and prayed together. They welcomed pilgrims and travellers, offering them protection and hospitality. The Templar commanderies, often associated with the fortresses, managed the surrounding lands, supporting the agricultural and economic activities that financed military campaigns.

The Fall of the Fortresses and the End of the Order.

With the end of the Crusades and the rise of Muslim forces, many Templar fortresses fell one after the other. The fall of Acre in 1291, the last Christian stronghold in the Holy Land, marked the end of an era. The fortresses, once symbols of indomitable resistance, were either destroyed or captured by Muslim forces.

The loss of the Templar fortresses also precipitated the dissolution of the order in Europe. The Templars, deprived of their strategic bastions, could not maintain their influence and power. In 1312, the order was officially dissolved by Pope Clement V, under pressure from King Philip IV of France.

Conclusion.

The Templar fortresses were much more than stone and mortar constructions; they were bastions of faith, resistance, and military ingenuity. Each wall, each tower, and each rampart carried within it the history of knights ready to sacrifice their lives to protect Christianity. Their strategic role in battles and sieges, as well as their symbolic impact, have left an indelible mark on the history of the Crusades. These fortresses, silent witnesses of a heroic past, continue to fascinate and inspire, reminding us of the ideals of bravery and devotion that animated the Templars.

Chapter 5: The Economy and Possessions of the Templars.

The Commanderies and Land Properties of the Templars.

In the maze of medieval paths, between fortified villages and vast plains, the commanderies of the Templars rose like beacons of power and piety. These establishments, both military bastions, economic centres and spiritual refuges, constituted the nervous system of the Order of the Poor Knights of Christ and of the Temple of Solomon. The commanderies, supported by extensive land holdings, formed the material base on which the sacred mission of the Templars rested.

The Foundation of the Commanderies.

The Templar commanderies emerged in the early 12th century, shortly after the creation of the order in 1119. Their rapid development was made possible thanks to the generous donations of land and goods by European nobles, eager to support the defenders of the Holy Land. These donations, often motivated by spiritual and political considerations, allowed the Templars to establish an extensive network of commanderies across Europe and the Levant.

Each commandery was led by a commander, an experienced and respected knight, responsible for managing the lands and resources. The commander reported to the provincial master, who oversaw the activities of several commanderies in a given region. This hierarchy ensured an efficient and centralized administration, essential to the prosperity of the order.

The Architecture and Function of Commanderies.

The commanderies were multifunctional structures, designed to meet the military, economic, and spiritual needs of the Templars. Their architecture varied depending on local resources and specific needs, but several elements were common to most commanderies.

The Fortifications: Many commanderies were fortified, with thick walls and watchtowers, allowing them to defend the places against attacks. These fortifications, although often modest compared to large fortresses, offered sufficient protection against local incursions and bandits.

The Chapel: At the heart of each commandery was a chapel, a place of prayer and contemplation for the knights. The chapel was a sacred sanctuary where the Templars gathered for religious services, thus renewing their spiritual commitment and seeking divine guidance in their daily actions.

The Dormitories and Refectories: The knights and sergeants resided in austere dormitories, reflecting their vow of poverty. Meals were taken communally in the refectories, in silence, often accompanied by pious readings. This communal life strengthened the bonds of fraternity and discipline among the members of the order.

The Stables and Workshops: The commanderies had stables for the knights' and sergeants' horses, essential for military missions and patrols. Workshops allowed for the manufacture and repair of weapons, armour, and equipment necessary for the Templars' military and daily life.

The Barns and Warehouses: The surrounding farmland was used to produce food and resources. The barns and warehouses stored the crops, wine, oil and other products, thus ensuring the self-sufficiency of the commandery and the ability to support military campaigns.

The Lands and Real Estate.

The Templars' land holdings were vast and diverse, including farmland, forests, vineyards, mills, and villages. These properties, often acquired through donation, inheritance, or purchase, constituted the material wealth of the order. The Templars administered these assets with exemplary rigor, maximizing returns and reinvesting profits into their missions.

Agricultural Lands: The vast agricultural lands produced wheat, barley, vegetables and other foodstuffs. The Templars introduced advanced agricultural techniques, such as three-field crop rotation and irrigation, to improve yields. The surplus production was sold on local markets, generating significant income for the order.

The Vineyards and Orchards: The vineyards, particularly in France and Spain, produced wine, a valuable and lucrative commodity. The Templars were also involved in the cultivation of orchards, producing fruits and essential oils. These products were used both for internal consumption and for trade.

Forests and Pastures: The forests provided construction and heating wood, while the pastures allowed for the breeding of cattle, sheep, and horses. Breeding was crucial for the production of meat, wool, and leather, as well as for maintaining sturdy mounts for the knights.

The Villages and the Mills.

The Templars also owned entire villages, where peasants worked the land in exchange for protection and support. These villages were prosperous communities, well managed by the Templars, who ensured justice and security for the inhabitants. The peasants, grateful for the protection offered, were loyal to the order and contributed to its wealth.

The mills, often located on rivers, were essential for grinding grain and producing flour. These mills, sometimes fortified, were vital economic centres, attracting nearby peasants to process their crops. The Templars collected royalties for the use of the mills, thus increasing their income.

The Rigorous and Efficient Management.

The management of land assets and commanderies was characterized by administrative rigor and methodical organization. The Templars kept precise records of their properties, yields, and transactions. Each commandery was autonomous in its daily management, but regularly reported to the provincial master and the Grand Master.

This efficient management allowed the Templars to maximize their resources and finance their military and charitable activities. The revenues from the commanderies supported the fortresses in the Holy Land, financed military expeditions, and maintained a Christian presence in hostile regions. The commanderies, far from being simple residences, were nerve centres of the Templar economy.

The Commanderies as Centres of Power.

The Templar commanderies were not only economic centres, but also places of power and influence. The Templars, respected for their integrity and competence, often played a role in local and regional politics. They served as mediators in conflicts, offered advice to local lords, and participated in the defence of territories against invasions.

Their extensive network of commanderies allowed the Templars to quickly move resources and troops, ensuring an effective response to threats. The commanderies, connected by secure routes and relays, facilitated communication and exchanges between different regions. This solid infrastructure strengthened the cohesion of the order and allowed for effective coordination of military and logistical operations.

Conclusion.

The commanderies and landed properties of the Templars were the foundations of their power and influence. These establishments, much more than simple properties, were centres of community life, economic management, and military preparation. The Templars, through their rigorous administration and commitment to the sacred mission, were able to transform these lands into bastions of Christianity.

Through the commanderies, the Templars left a lasting legacy of discipline, devotion, and ingenuity. Their network of land holdings and administrative centres supported their efforts in the Holy Land and allowed the order to prosper for nearly two centuries. The Templar commanderies, symbols of their faith and mission, continue to fascinate with their history and their impact on the medieval world.

Banking and Economic Activities of the Templars.

In the austere corridors of their commanderies and under the vaults of their chapels, the Templars were not content with forging swords and polishing armour. They also forged powerful economic networks and set up innovative banking systems that would transform the trade and finances of medieval Europe. These knights, whose sacred duty was to protect pilgrims and holy places, also became the guardians and facilitators of wealth, weaving a web of economic influence that extended from the shores of the Mediterranean to the royal courts of Europe.

Origins of Banking Activities.

The banking activities of the Templars took root in their logistical and military needs. The high cost of the Crusades and the need to finance fortresses and expeditions in the Holy Land pushed them to develop methods to manage and transfer funds in a secure and efficient manner. Donations and bequests from European nobles significantly increased the wealth of the order, requiring sophisticated financial management.

The Bills of Exchange.

The Templars were among the first to use bills of exchange, a revolutionary financial instrument that allowed the transfer of funds without carrying gold or silver, thus reducing the risk of theft. A noble wishing to travel to the Holy Land could deposit his funds in a Templar commandery in Europe and receive a bill of exchange which he would present to a commandery in the East to withdraw the equivalent in local currency.

This system of bills of exchange offered unprecedented security to travellers and pilgrims, while facilitating international trade. The Templars, thanks to their well-established and secure network of commanderies, could guarantee the validity and security of these transactions, thus becoming the bankers of medieval Europe.

Deposits and Loans.

In addition to bills of exchange, the Templars accepted deposits of money and valuable objects. Nobles and kings entrusted their treasures to the Templars, knowing that the order's fortresses offered greater security than the chests of their own castles. In return, the Templars issued detailed receipts of the deposits, creating an early form of deposit bank.

The Templars also granted loans, often at moderate interest rates. Kings, nobles, and merchants turned to them to finance their military campaigns, commercial ventures, or construction projects. These loans were secured by land assets or future revenues, thus ensuring a return on investment for the order. Sometimes, these loans gave the Templars considerable power over the debtors, strengthening their political and economic influence.

Management of Lands and Properties.

The vast land holdings of the Templars were managed with remarkable efficiency. Each commandery functioned as an autonomous economic unit, exploiting agricultural lands, forests, vineyards and pastures. Agricultural products and manufactured goods were traded on local and international markets, generating substantial revenues.

The commanderies sold their production surpluses and bought necessary goods for their subsistence and military activities. The Templars actively participated in trade fairs, using their network to buy and sell products across Europe and the Levant. Their ability to produce, store and distribute essential goods allowed them to maintain a robust and self-sufficient economy.

Role in International Trade.

The Templar network extended from the ports of the Mediterranean to the commercial centres of continental Europe, facilitating international trade. The Templars owned ships and warehouses in strategic ports, allowing them to control sea routes and transport goods safely. They imported spices, silks, precious stones and other valuable goods from the East, which they resold in Europe at high prices.

Their involvement in international trade went beyond simple logistics. The Templars were also savvy investors, financing commercial expeditions and mercantile ventures. Their expertise in trade and finance allowed them to advise and support merchants and businesses, thus promoting the economic growth of medieval Europe.

Influence on Kings and States.

Their wealth and financial expertise gave the Templars considerable influence over kings and European states. They became the financial advisors of the sovereigns, offering loans to finance wars, construction projects, and court needs. In return, they received privileges, tax exemptions, and lands.

This symbiotic relationship with the monarchs strengthened their political power. The Templars could, if necessary, mobilize financial and military resources quickly, making them indispensable allies. Their network of commanderies also served as espionage and diplomacy centres, gathering crucial information and facilitating negotiations between states.

The Tomb of Riches and the Enigma of Dissolution.

The wealth accumulated by the Templars, combined with their increasing influence, aroused envy and suspicion. At the beginning of the 14th century, King Philip IV of France, heavily indebted to the order, sought to seize their assets. Accusing the Templars of heresy and various crimes, he obtained the dissolution of the order in 1312 by Pope Clement V. The Templars' assets were confiscated, and their leaders were arrested and executed.

However, the dissolution of the order did not put an end to their legend. The treasures of the Templars, supposedly hidden or dispersed before their arrest, fuelled myths and speculations for centuries. Their financial expertise and economic network continued to influence banking and commercial systems long after their official disappearance.

Economic Heritage.

The economic legacy of the Templars is immense. They laid the foundations of modern banking practices, such as bills of exchange, deposits and secured loans. Their rigorous approach to land and property management influenced agricultural and commercial methods. Their role in international trade and the finances of European states contributed to the emergence of a more integrated and dynamic medieval economy.

The Templars, through their innovation and discipline, demonstrated that even in a world dominated by war and faith, economic prosperity could be achieved and maintained. Their management model and financial network continue to inspire and intrigue, symbolizing the unique alliance of piety, courage, and ingenuity.

Conclusion.

The banking and economic activities of the Templars were an essential pillar of their power and influence. Through their ability to manage considerable resources and innovate in the financial field, they left a lasting imprint on the medieval economy. Their network of commanderies and their financial expertise allowed the order to support its military and charitable missions, while playing a central role in European trade and politics. The Templars, both warriors and bankers, embodied an ideal where faith and reason, strength and ingenuity, came together to shape history.

Economic Influence of the Templars in Europe and the East.

Under the Gothic arches of European cathedrals and in the imposing shadow of the Holy Land fortresses, the economic influence of the Templars extended, weaving a complex network that connected the Christian West to the Muslim East. Their presence was not only marked by the crusades and battles, but also by a robust economy that supported their military and charitable efforts. The Order of the Poor Knights of Christ and of the Temple of Solomon became a major player in the medieval economy, influencing trade, finance, and politics of European kingdoms and Latin states of the East.

Expansion and Management of Land Assets.

The vast land holdings of the Templars constituted the basis of their economic influence. From their foundation, European nobles and monarchs granted them lands, castles, and villages in exchange for the protection of pilgrims and holy places. These gifts, often motivated by spiritual and strategic considerations, allowed the Templars to build up an impressive land estate.

Each Templar commandery functioned as an autonomous economic unit, managing its lands with remarkable efficiency. The Templars introduced advanced agricultural techniques, improving yields and diversifying crops. The lands produced wheat, barley, vegetables, fruits and wine, while the forests and pastures provided wood, wool and livestock. Surplus products were sold on local markets, generating substantial revenues that financed their military and charitable activities.

Network of Commanderies and Trade.

The network of Templar commanderies, extending from Western Europe to the Holy Land, facilitated trade and exchanges. The commanderies were often located along trade routes and pilgrimage paths, serving as relay points for travellers and merchants. The Templars developed infrastructures such as bridges, roads and inns, improving communications and transport.

The Templars actively participated in international trade, using their ships and warehouses located in strategic ports of the Mediterranean. They imported spices, silks, precious stones and other valuable goods from the East, which they resold in Europe at high prices. Their ability to transport goods safely, thanks to their network of well-defended fortresses and ships, made them reliable and sought-after trading partners.

Banking and Financial Activities.

One of the most significant contributions of the Templars to the medieval economy was innovation in banking and financial practices. The need to finance the Crusades and manage the considerable donations received by the order pushed them to develop methods to secure and transfer funds. The Templars introduced letters of exchange, allowing money to be transferred without carrying gold or silver, thus reducing the risk of theft.

The Templars also offered deposit and loan services, accepting money and valuable items in secure deposit. Nobles and kings entrusted their treasures to the Templars, knowing that their fortresses offered superior security. In return, the Templars issued receipts and letters of credit, creating an early form of deposit bank. They also granted loans at moderate interest rates, supporting the military, commercial, and construction projects of kings and nobles.

Influence on Monarchs and States.

The wealth and financial expertise of the Templars gave them considerable influence over monarchs and European states. They became the financial advisors of sovereigns, offering loans to finance wars, crusades and economic ventures. In return, they received privileges, tax exemptions and lands, strengthening their economic and political power.

The Templars also played a crucial role in diplomacy and politics. Their network of commanderies and their relationships with monarchs allowed them to serve as mediators and negotiators in conflicts. They could quickly mobilize financial and military resources, making them indispensable allies in struggles for power and territories.

The Impact in the East.

In the East, the Templars were pillars of Christian presence, supporting the Latin states and the fortresses that defended the holy places. Their economic influence in the East was based on their ability to finance and support fortresses, garrisons, and military expeditions. The Templars managed lands and local resources, contributing to the economy of the Latin states.

Their fortresses, such as the Krak des Chevaliers, Château Pèlerin and Safed, were economic centres in addition to being military bastions. The Templars collected taxes and fees from local peasants and traders, thus financing their military operations and charitable works. Their presence in the East also facilitated trade between the West and the East, creating economic ties that strengthened the stability of the Latin states.

Economic Legacy of the Templars.

The economic legacy of the Templars is immense and enduring. Their network of commanderies, their innovative banking practices, and their role in international trade have left an indelible imprint on the medieval economy. They demonstrated that military power and economic prosperity could go hand in hand, and that faith could be a driver of economic development.

The Templars, through their discipline, ingenuity, and devotion, created a robust economy that supported their spiritual and military missions. Their economic influence, both in Europe and the East, attests to their ability to adapt and innovate in diverse and often hostile contexts. Their management model and financial network continue to inspire and intrigue, symbolizing the unique alliance of piety, courage, and ingenuity.

Conclusion.

The economic influence of the Templars extended well beyond their military exploits. Their network of commanderies, their efficient management of land assets, and their banking innovations placed them at the heart of the medieval economy. By weaving links between Europe and the East, supporting monarchs and states, and innovating in financial practices, the Templars left an economic legacy that continues to fascinate. Their ability to combine faith, economy, and power remains an example of the profound impact that well-managed and high-ideal inspired institutions can have.

Chapter 6: The Decline and Fall of the Order.

Conflicts with European Sovereigns.

In the shadows of their fortresses and the halls of palaces, the Order of the Templars, once revered and powerful, began to face increasing tensions with European sovereigns. These conflicts, fuelled by envy, suspicion and political intrigue, intensified over time, precipitating the decline of the order. The once cordial relations deteriorated into a fierce struggle for power, resources and influence.

The Roots of Tensions.

At the height of their power, the Templars possessed immense wealth, vast lands, and a network of commanderies extending across Europe and the Holy Land. Their independence, guaranteed by papal bulls, allowed them to operate without the intervention of local authorities or feudal lords. This autonomy, so precious for the effectiveness of their mission, became a source of tension with European sovereigns.

Kings and lords, faced with constant financial challenges, looked enviously at the vast treasures and properties of the Templars. Their tax-exempt status, granted by the Pope, meant that the order's wealth escaped the royal coffers, exacerbating the resentment of the monarchs. The order, although faithful to its religious and military mission, found itself increasingly at odds with the secular interests of its initial benefactors.

Philip IV of France and the Stakes of Power.

King Philip IV of France, nicknamed Philip the Fair, played a central role in escalating conflicts with the Templars. Known for his ambition and desire to centralize power, Philip was also faced with growing financial difficulties. His costly wars and expansionist policies had left him in debt, including to the Templars, who often served as bankers to European kings.

Philippe saw the wealth of the Templars as a solution to his financial problems. Moreover, their growing power and political influence made him suspicious. The Templars had close diplomatic relations with other European monarchies and maintained a certain independence from the French crown. This independence was perceived by Philippe as a threat to his authority.

The First Frictions.

The first frictions between Philippe and the Templars appeared during his attempts to tax ecclesiastical goods. Although the Templars were technically exempt from such taxes by papal decrees, Philippe was looking for ways to circumvent these protections. His efforts to impose taxes on Templar properties were strongly contested, leading to increasing tensions.

Philippe also used the courts to attack the order, seeking legal pretexts to confiscate their property. The Templars resisted these attempts, but each confrontation strengthened the king's animosity. The order, faithful to its vow of obedience to the pope, found itself in a delicate position, navigating between ecclesiastical loyalty and royal pressure.

The Accusations and the Conspiracy.

Tensions reached their peak in 1307, when Philippe implemented a bold plan to destroy the order. Under the pretext of serious accusations of heresy, blasphemy, and moral corruption, Philippe ordered the arrest of all the Templars in France on Friday, October 13, 1307. This fateful date marked the beginning of the end for the order.

The accusations, although shocking, were based on rumours and testimonies extorted under torture. Philippe, determined to eliminate the Templars as an obstacle to his power, manipulated public opinion and used the tools of the Inquisition to pursue his goal. The knights, once respected and admired, were suddenly presented as deviants and traitors to the Christian faith.

The Reaction of Other European Sovereigns.

The reaction of other European sovereigns to Philip's attack on the Templars was varied. Some, like King Edward II of England, were initially reluctant to follow Philip's example. Edward had benefited from the financial and military services of the Templars and was sceptical about the accusations against them. However, under pressure from Pope Clement V and facing internal political tensions, he eventually consented to similar actions against the order in England.

Other monarchs, seeing an opportunity to seize the Templars' assets, followed Philippe's example with more eagerness. In Spain and Portugal, the Templars' assets were confiscated, and their members arrested, although the charges brought against them were often less severe than those in France. In these regions, the Templars enjoyed some support among the population and the nobility, complicating efforts to persecute them.

The Role of Pope Clement V.

Pope Clement V, caught between Philip's ambitions and his spiritual responsibilities, played a crucial role in the fate of the Templars. Although reluctant to approve Philip's actions, Clement found himself in a position of political weakness. The relocation of the papacy to Avignon, under French influence, weakened papal authority and made it more susceptible to royal pressures.

Clément, seeking to maintain the unity of the Church and to avoid a schism, eventually yielded to Philippe's demands. In 1312, at the Council of Vienne, he pronounced the official dissolution of the Templar order, transferring their assets to the Hospitallers. This decision, although driven by political considerations, was a fatal blow to the order.

The Consequences and the Decline.

The destruction of the Templars by Philip IV had profound and lasting consequences. The fall of the order, once so powerful and respected, sent a clear message about the fragility of institutions in the face of political ambition. The economic and military network of the Templars was dismantled, and their fortresses and assets were redistributed.

Their decline also marked the end of an era of crusades and expeditions to the Holy Land. The Templars had been among the most fervent defenders of the Latin states of the East, and their disappearance further weakened the Christian position in the Holy Land.

Conclusion.

Conflicts with European sovereigns, particularly with Philip IV of France, precipitated the decline and fall of the Templars. These tensions, rooted in envy and political ambitions, showed the vulnerability of a powerful order to royal machinations. The Templars, despite their bravery and devotion, were ultimately victims of political intrigue and greed, leaving behind a legacy of mystery and legend. Their story remains a poignant testament to the destructive forces of jealousy and power, and the tragedies that can ensue.

The Arrest Warrant and the Day of Friday, October 13, 1307.

Under a leaden sky, in the cold and misty dawn of a fateful day, the history of the Templars changed forever. On Friday, October 13, 1307, a date that would forever mark the annals of time, King Philip IV of France implemented a Machiavellian plan to destroy the Order of the Poor Knights of Christ and of the Temple of Solomon. This day, which began like so many others for the Templars, turned into an unprecedented betrayal, sealing the fate of these sacred warriors.

The Intrigue of Philippe le Bel.

Philippe IV, nicknamed Philippe le Bel, was a king known for his determination and cold ambition. Indebted to the Templars, envious of their wealth and suspicious of their power, he hatched a plot to seize their assets and annihilate their influence. The preparations were long and meticulous, marked by rumours and suspicions, while Philippe quietly gathered the pieces of his deadly chess game.

Philippe skilfully used accusations of heresy, blasphemy, and moral corruption to justify his actions. He manipulated public opinion and religious authorities, convincing Pope Clement V of the need for an investigation. However, Philippe had already made his decision and planned every detail of the massive arrest of the Templars.

The Arrest Warrant.

The arrest warrant, signed by Philippe IV and sealed by his council, was secretly sent to all the bailiffs and seneschals of the kingdom. These orders, kept under the utmost secrecy, were to be executed simultaneously across France at dawn on Friday, October 13, 1307. The bailiffs and seneschals were instructed to proceed with the arrest of all the Templars, seize their assets, and confiscate their properties.

The Templars, oblivious to the brewing storm, went about their daily tasks. They prayed in their chapels, maintained their weapons, and managed their lands with the same discipline and devotion that had characterized their order since its foundation. Their commanderies, scattered throughout France, were bastions of peace and faith, suddenly threatened by insidious betrayal.

The Night Before the Arrest.

On the night of October 12, a deceptive calm enveloped the Templar commanderies. The knights, sergeants, and lay brothers slept peacefully, unaware of the imminent danger. The commanderies, although fortified, were not prepared for the assault that was to come from within the very kingdom they had sworn to protect.

In Paris, Jacques de Molay, the Grand Master of the Templars, was immersed in prayer and reflection. Having recently participated in discussions with the king and the pope, he was concerned about rumours of heresy accusations, but did not suspect the extent of the conspiracy being plotted against him and his brothers.

The Dawn of Friday the 13th of October.

When the grey dawn of Friday, October 13th rose, the royal bailiffs and seneschals put the secret orders into action. Throughout all of France, the doors of the commanderies were broken down, the Templars surprised in their sleep, often without the slightest time to defend themselves. The knights, trained to confront enemies on the battlefield, found themselves unarmed in the face of this internal attack.

In Paris, Jacques de Molay was arrested along with his closest advisors. The Templars, incredulous, were chained and dragged out of their commanderies, their weapons and possessions seized in front of the local populations, often stunned by this sudden violence against men considered as the protectors of the faith.

The Accusations.

The charges brought against the Templars were serious and numerous. Philippe accused them of denying Christ, spitting on the cross, practicing obscene rites, and engaging in immoral acts. These accusations, based on confessions extorted under torture, were used to justify the arrest and confiscation of Templar property.

The Grand Master Jacques de Molay and the other leaders were subjected to brutal interrogations. Under torture, confessions were extorted, although many Templars vehemently denied the accusations, preferring to suffer rather than betray their vows and their faith.

The Reaction in Europe.

The news of the massive arrest of the Templars spread quickly across Europe, causing shock and outrage. European sovereigns, although initially hesitant, were forced to follow Philippe's example under the pressure of Pope Clement V, who, albeit reluctantly, supported the actions of the King of France to avoid a schism.

In England, in Spain, in Germany and in other kingdoms, the Templars were also arrested and their assets confiscated. However, in some regions, the Templars received stronger support, and the accusations were treated with more scepticism. The commanderies of the Iberian Peninsula, for example, continued to resist and defend their honour fiercely.

The Immediate Consequences.

The arrest of the Templars led to immediate and devastating consequences for the order. Their assets were seized and redistributed, mainly to the Hospitallers. The knights, once powerful and respected, were humiliated and imprisoned, many succumbing to the tortures inflicted to obtain confessions.

The people, witnessing this dramatic fall, were torn between belief in the accusations made against the Templars and suspicion towards King Philip's motivations. The churches, chapels and Templar properties, once places of prayer and safety, became symbols of betrayal and royal greed.

The Symbolism of Friday the 13th.

Friday, October 13, 1307 became a symbol of bad luck and tragedy, a superstition that still persists today. This fateful day, which saw the fall of one of the most powerful and respected orders of Christendom, marked the end of an era and the beginning of the darkening of the Templar legend. The knights, once heroes of the crusades, were reduced to shadows, their exploits eclipsed by political machinations.

The Memory of the Templars.

The memory of the Templars, tarnished by accusations and tortures, however survived through the centuries. Their history, marked by courage, devotion and tragedy, continued to inspire and fascinate.

The mysteries surrounding their arrest and disappearance fuelled legends, myths and speculations about their hidden treasures and lost secrets.

The Accusations and Torture of the Templars.

At the heart of the intrigues and machinations of the kingdom of France, a conspiracy hatched by King Philip IV and his council was taking shape. The Templars, once revered as the defenders of Christendom, suddenly found themselves plunged into an abyss of slander and suffering. The accusations levelled against them, although shaped by treachery and greed, were of such gravity and scope that they would seal their fate. This dark chapter in the history of the Templars, marked by torture and extorted confessions, still resonates as a cry of injustice through the centuries.

The Arrest and the Betrayal.

On Friday, October 13, 1307, the Templars were arrested en masse throughout all of France. The knights, seized in their commanderies, were chained and taken to cold and dark cells, where they would be subjected to ruthless interrogations. The arrest order, signed by Philippe IV, marked the beginning of a campaign of terror and brutality.

The interrogations were conducted by royal inquisitors, often in the presence of representatives from the ecclesiastical Inquisition. The methods used to obtain confessions were as cruel as they were inhumane. Torture, authorized by the papacy for cases of heresy, became the main instrument for extracting confessions from the knights.

Torture: Instruments of Terror.

The Templars, subjected to indescribable sufferings, were confronted with the most horrifying torture instruments. The rack, the strappado, the water torture and other infernal devices were used to break their will and spirit. The screams of the knights echoed in the dungeons, a sinister echo of human barbarity.

The rack, a wooden frame where victims were stretched to the point of dislocating their limbs, was particularly dreaded. Tendons would tear, bones would crack, and the pain was unbearable. Under this torture, even the bravest souls often found themselves unable to resist.

The strappado, where prisoners were suspended by their wrists behind their back and brutally released, caused dislocations and muscle tears. This torture, repeated several times, left lasting physical and psychological aftereffects.

The water torture, a precursor to the modern waterboarding technique, involved forcing victims to swallow large amounts of water, causing suffocation and extreme distress. The knights, deprived of air and hope, choked under the pressure of the water, their minds wavering between consciousness and unconsciousness.

The Extorted Confessions.

Under torture, some Templars, unable to bear the pain, ended up confessing to the crimes they were accused of. These confessions, often incoherent and contradictory, were extracted in a state of extreme distress. The knights, physically and mentally broken, confessed everything their tormentors wanted to hear, hoping to put an end to their unbearable suffering.

Jacques de Molay, the Grand Master of the Templars, was also subjected to torture. Under inhumane pressure, he confessed to acts of heresy which he later denied, asserting that his confessions had been forced. His retraction, like that of many other Templars, could not however undo the impact of the initial confessions obtained under torture.

Propaganda and Public Opinion.

The extorted confessions were used by Philippe IV to justify his actions to Pope Clement V and the public opinion. Pamphlets and proclamations were distributed throughout the kingdom, recounting the confessions of the Templars and describing them as monsters and heretics. The royal propaganda, skilfully orchestrated, transformed the knights, once revered, into outcasts of society.

The Church, although initially sceptical, found itself forced by confessions and political pressures to support the king's action. Pope Clement V, despite his doubts and hesitations, eventually gave in, convening a council to examine the accusations and confessions of the Templars. The inquisitorial machine, once launched, was difficult to stop, and the Templars, despite their innocence, were trapped in a relentless spiral.

The Resistance and the Dignity.

Despite the tortures and sufferings, some Templars resisted with remarkable dignity. Refusing to renounce their faith and their order, they endured the torments with stoic courage. Their resistance became a symbol of their integrity and their dedication to their vows.

The testimonies of those who resisted, although few in number, echoed through the centuries as a reminder of the strength of the human spirit in the face of cruelty. These knights, martyrs of betrayal and injustice, embodied the true essence of the Templars: unwavering faith and indomitable courage.

The Legacy of Torture.

The tortures inflicted on the Templars left indelible scars, not only on the bodies of the victims, but also on the soul of medieval Europe. The brutality of the methods used and the injustice of the accusations tarnished the reputation of ecclesiastical and royal justice. The Templars, although destroyed as an order, became symbols of persecution and resistance to oppression.

The history of the accusations and torture of the Templars is a dark chapter that reminds us of the dangers of absolute power and political manipulation. It teaches us the fragility of institutions in the face of excessive ambitions and the necessity to defend justice and truth, even against the most formidable forces.

The Trials of the Templars in France.

When the dawn of justice rose over the kingdom of France, the shadows of the Templars stood in the cold and austere halls of the courts. The Knights Templar were faced with a series of infamous trials. These trials, marked by betrayal, manipulation and torture, remain one of the darkest chapters in judicial history.

The Beginning of the Trials.

The trials of the Templars began shortly after their arrest. Philip IV, determined to justify his actions and legitimize the seizure of the order's assets, undertook to publicly demonstrate the guilt of the Templars. The king used the Inquisition, an ecclesiastical court, to conduct investigations and interrogate the accused. Under the authority of the Bishop of Sens, Philippe de Marigny, and Guillaume de Nogaret, the Templars were subjected to intense and often brutal interrogations.

The hearings took place in various locations, including Paris, at the Château de Chinon, and in other cities where Templar commanderies had been seized. The judges, representatives of the Inquisition and the crown, were determined to obtain confessions, whatever the method.

The Accusations Made.

The accusations against the Templars were numerous and serious. They were accused of heresy, witchcraft, obscene practices, and treason. More specifically, the Templars were accused of denying Christ, spitting on the cross, worshipping a pagan idol called Baphomet, and engaging in depraved initiation rites. The testimonies, often obtained under torture, described scenes of debauchery and sacrilege that horrified the judges and the public.

These accusations, although spectacular, lacked concrete evidence. Confessions extracted under torture were often inconsistent and contradictory. However, in the climate of fear and suspicion that prevailed, these details mattered little. The purpose of the trials was not so much to discover the truth as to provide a legal justification for the destruction of the order and the confiscation of its wealth.

The Judicial Procedures.

The judicial procedures were often summary and biased. The Templars, deprived of their defence rights, had little means to contest the accusations. The judges, under the influence of Philip IV, were determined to obtain convictions. Torture, authorized by the Pope for cases of heresy, was systematically used to extort confessions.

The interrogations were conducted under deplorable conditions. The Templars, weakened by months of imprisonment and mistreatment, were often unable to physically and mentally resist the pressures exerted on them. The accounts of the interrogations reveal scenes of cruelty where the accused, chained and tortured, ended up confessing everything they were asked.

The Declarations of Jacques de Molay.

Jacques de Molay, the Grand Master of the Templars, was one of the central figures in the trials. Arrested in Paris and subjected to torture, he initially confessed to some of the crimes he was accused of. However, during his public appearance, Jacques de Molay retracted, stating that his confessions had been obtained under duress and that he had never betrayed his faith or his order.

His retraction, although courageous, had little impact on the course of events. The judges, under the influence of Philip IV, continued to present the initial confessions as irrefutable evidence of the Templars' guilt. Jacques de Molay's determination to defend the honour of his order until the end remains a poignant testament to his bravery and loyalty.

The Testimonies and the Confessions.

The trials of the Templars were marked by a multitude of testimonies and confessions. The knights, subjected to torture, described scenes that seemed to come from the imagination of the inquisitors. The confessions were often similar, suggesting that the interrogators had prepared the questions and answers in advance. The Templars, under duress, found themselves confirming accusations they knew to be false, but which they could not refute without enduring further suffering.

Some Templars, despite the tortures, continued to deny the accusations. Their resistance, although noble, could not prevent the judges from declaring them guilty. The majority of the Templars, exhausted by the tortures and incessant interrogations, ended up yielding, thus adding to the pile of confessions that justified the condemnation of the order.

The Role of Pope Clement V.

Pope Clement V, although reluctant to fully support the actions of Philip IV, was forced by political pressures and the delicate situation of the papacy. Residing in Avignon under French influence, Clement V tried to play both sides. He ordered a parallel papal investigation and convened a council to discuss the charges brought against the Templars.

The Council of Vienne, in 1312, resulted in the official dissolution of the Order of the Templars. Clement V, seeking to preserve the unity of the Church and to avoid open conflict with Philip IV, accepted the results of the investigations conducted under torture. The assets of the Templars were transferred to the Order of the Hospitallers, although Philip IV ensured he retained a large portion of the confiscated wealth in France.

The Executions and the Fate of the Templars.

The trials of the Templars ended with severe sentences. Many Templars were executed, burned alive on public pyres. On March 18, 1314, Jacques de Molay and Geoffroy de Charnay, the Preceptor of Normandy, were led to the Jews' Island, on the Seine, in Paris. There, in front of a gathered crowd, they were burned alive after proclaiming their innocence and denouncing the injustices they were victims of.

Their death, although tragic, marked the symbolic end of the Templar order. The flames that consumed their bodies illuminated the Parisian night, leaving an indelible imprint on the collective imagination.

The last words of Jacques de Molay, calling Philippe IV and Clement V to appear before the divine tribunal, resonated like a prophetic curse.

The Trials of the Templars in Other Countries.

Beyond the borders of France, the fall of the Templars resonated throughout Europe, leading to trials in several kingdoms. Although the events varied in intensity and method, the persecution of the Knights Templar extended well beyond the machinations of Philip IV. Other nations, influenced by political and religious pressures, were swept up in a wave of arrests and trials, each tinged with local nuances of justice and power.

England.

In England, the Templars enjoyed some initial protection under the reign of King Edward II, who was hesitant to follow the brutal actions of his French counterpart. Edward, aware of the usefulness of the Templars and their financial services, showed restraint despite the pressures from Pope Clement V.

However, under the increasing pressure from the papacy and King Philip IV, Edward eventually gave in. In January 1308, the Templars were arrested in England, although the legal proceedings were less severe than those in France. Accusations of heresy and immoral practices were made, but the methods of torture, common in France, were largely avoided.

The trials took place mainly in London, where the Templars were questioned. The confessions were obtained without the cruelties inflicted in France, and many knights denied the accusations, asserting their innocence. Edward II, beset by internal political problems, was not as zealous as Philip IV in the persecution of the order. Eventually, the Templars' assets were confiscated and transferred to the Order of the Hospitallers, but the knights themselves were treated with relative leniency.

Spain and Portugal.

In Spain, the kingdoms of Castile, Aragon, and Navarre reacted differently to the fall of the Templars. The Knights Templar enjoyed considerable support in the Iberian Peninsula due to their crucial role in the Reconquista against the Moors. The Spanish kings were reluctant to persecute an order that had significantly contributed to the Christian defence.

King James II of Aragon initiated investigations into the Templars, but the trials were conducted with scepticism and reluctance. Testimonies obtained under torture in France were received with suspicion, and accusations of heresy were difficult to prove. The Spanish Templars, although arrested, were often released due to lack of conclusive evidence.

In Castile, King Ferdinand IV adopted a similar approach, ordering investigations but avoiding brutal methods of torture. The Templars were judged with a certain leniency, and many were acquitted or received light sentences.

In Portugal, King Denis I showed notable support for the Templars. Recognizing their military and economic importance, he refused to persecute the order with the same intensity as Philip IV. In 1319, after the dissolution of the order by the Pope, Denis I created the Order of Christ, allowing the Portuguese Templars to join this new institution. This move allowed their legacy and influence in Portugal to be preserved.

Germany.

In Germany, the Templars were less numerous and less influential than in France or Spain. Nevertheless, the calls to action by Philip IV and Pope Clement V found an echo among the princes and prelates of the Holy Roman Empire. Arrests began in 1308, but the trials were often delayed by the internal political divisions of the Empire.

The trials of the Templars in Germany were characterized by less use of torture and greater caution in judgments. The German princes, less dependent on the papacy than Philip IV, did not have the same motivations to destroy the order. The charges brought against the Templars were examined with scepticism, and many knights were acquitted.

However, in certain regions, the Templars' assets were confiscated and redistributed, often to the Hospitallers or local lords. The dissolution of the order in Germany, although less brutal, nevertheless marked the end of their influence in the region.

Italy.

In Italy, the trials of the Templars were marked by political fragmentation and the diverging interests of various city-states and kingdoms. The Papal States, under the direct influence of the papacy, were among the first to act. Pope Clement V, residing in Avignon, ordered investigations and arrests in the territories under his control.

The Italian Templars, although subjected to interrogations, did not undergo the same levels of torture as in France. The trials were conducted with some rigor, but the Italian judges remained divided on the guilt of the order. In some cities, the Templars were acquitted or released due to lack of conclusive evidence.

In Florence, Venice, and other city-states, local authorities took a more independent approach. Aware of the economic and military significance of the Templars, they were reluctant to persecute them harshly. Trials often ended in acquittals or light sentences, and the Templars' assets were typically confiscated and redistributed.

Other Regions.

In other regions of Europe, such as Hungary, Poland, and Scandinavia, the Templars were less numerous and less influential. Nevertheless, the calls from the papacy and Philip IV found an echo, and investigations were conducted. The results varied, but in many cases, the Templars were treated with a certain leniency.

The Dissolution of the Order by the Pope.

Under the troubled sky of medieval Europe, the order of the Templars, once valiant and honoured, found itself on the brink of annihilation. The flames of injustice licked the walls of their commanderies, and the whispers of betrayal echoed in the corridors of power. At the centre of this turmoil was Pope Clement V, whose decision to dissolve the order would mark one of the darkest chapters in Christian history.

Pope Clement V: Between the Hammer and the Anvil.

Clément V, elected pope in 1305, found himself in a precarious position. The seat of the papacy, recently moved to Avignon, was under the direct influence of Philip IV. The pope, although hesitant, could not ignore the intense pressures exerted by the king of France. Aware of the consequences of a direct confrontation with Philip, Clément found himself obliged to navigate cautiously between royal demands and the pursuit of truth.

From the beginning of the accusations, Clément V tried to take a measured position. He ordered an independent papal investigation, hoping to control the excesses of the French procedures. However, the testimonies obtained under torture in France weighed heavily in the balance, and the pope, despite his doubts, could not ignore the repeated confessions of sacrilege and heresy.

The Council of Vienna: The Final Judgment.

The Council of Vienne, convened by Clement V in 1311, was the stage where the fate of the Templars was played out. Prelates and dignitaries from all over Christendom gathered to discuss the accusations and the fate of the order. Philip IV, determined to see his will triumph, sent his emissaries to influence the deliberations.

The debates were intense and often stormy. The defenders of the Templars, though numerous, were confronted with the reality of confessions obtained under torture and the political manoeuvres of the

King of France. Clement V, caught in the vice of royal pressure and ecclesiastical interests, had to face a heartbreaking decision.

On March 22, 1312, Clement V, after careful consideration and under the constraint of circumstances, pronounced the dissolution of the Order of the Templars by the bull "Vox in excelso". This decision, although presented as a necessary measure for the good of the Church, was above all an act of submission to political demands. The dissolution of the order was a pragmatic response to the unbearable tensions that threatened to tear apart the unity of Christendom.

The Justifications for Dissolution.

Clément V justified the dissolution with a series of legal and doctrinal considerations. The bull "Vox in excelso" explained that, although the evidence of the Templars' heresy was insufficient for a definitive conviction, the order had lost its reputation and credibility in the eyes of the Christian world. To preserve the honour of the Church and avoid further divisions, it was deemed necessary to suppress the order.

This decision, although marked by pragmatism, left a bitter taste of injustice. The Templars, who had sacrificed so many lives for the defence of Christendom, were condemned not by irrefutable evidence, but by political necessity and the manipulation of confessions.

The Distribution of Templar Goods.

The dissolution of the order also raised the crucial question of the redistribution of its vast assets. Clement V, by the bull "Ad providam" promulgated on May 2, 1312, ordered that the properties of the Templars be transferred to the Order of the Hospitallers of Saint John of Jerusalem. This measure aimed to ensure that the resources once dedicated to the defence of the holy places continued to serve the same cause.

However, this redistribution was not without difficulties. In many territories, local lords and kings, attracted by the Templar wealth, resisted the transfer of goods to the Hospitallers. Philip IV, in particular, ensured that France kept a large part of the Templar treasures, using various pretexts to circumvent the papal decrees.

The Memory of the Templars.

The dissolution of the order left a void and a deep wound in the soul of Christendom. The Knights Templar, who had embodied the ideal of the crusader and defender of the faith, disappeared as an institution, but their memory survived. The brutality of their fall, the unfounded accusations and the confessions obtained under torture fuelled legends and myths.

The last grand master, Jacques de Molay, burned alive in 1314, proclaimed his innocence and cursed his persecutors, Philippe IV and Clément V, before succumbing to the flames. His heroic and tragic death cemented the image of the Templars as martyrs of injustice and royal greed.

The Legacy of Dissolution.

The legacy of the dissolution of the Templars is complex and multifaceted. On one hand, it reveals the fragility of institutions in the face of political intrigues and thirst for power. On the other hand, it highlights the resilience and transformation capacity of chivalrous ideals.

The Order of the Hospitallers, although different from the Templars, continued their mission of defence and charity, thus perpetuating a part of their legacy. In Portugal, the Order of Christ became the custodian of Templar traditions, transforming the tragedy of dissolution into a new chapter of service and devotion.

Conclusion.

The dissolution of the Templar Order by Pope Clement V was an act of political pragmatism dictated by the tumultuous circumstances of the time. Under pressure from Philip IV and facing the challenges of the Church's unity, Clement V made a decision that, although necessary to preserve peace, was marked by injustice and manipulation.

The Templars, despite their disappearance as an order, left a lasting legacy of courage, faith, and mystery. Their history, marked by sacrifice and persecution, continues to inspire and fascinate. The dissolution of the order, far from ending their legend, opened a new chapter of memory and reflection on justice, faith, and power.

The Flight of the Templars to Portugal and Scotland.

Under the dark skies of medieval Europe, as the flames of the pyres lit up the public squares and the shadow of Philip the Fair extended over the order of the Templars, some perspicacious and determined Templar knights managed to escape the claws of persecution. Their flight led them to more clement lands, where the aura of injustice would not reach them. Among these sanctuaries, Portugal and Scotland became havens of peace for these souls in search of refuge.

Tomar: The Knights' Rest in Portugal.

Portugal, under the wise and pragmatic governance of King Denis I, offered a welcome asylum to the persecuted Templars. This monarch, aware of the strategic and economic value of the knights, was not blinded by the defamatory accusations propagated by Philip IV and his minions. Thus, while persecution reached its peak in France, Denis I was discreetly preparing the ground to welcome these landless warriors.

In Tomar, a fortified city located in the heart of Portugal, the Templars found a safe refuge. The city, already marked by the Templar presence with its impressive fortress and its convent, became a bastion of resistance against oblivion. The fortress of Tomar, with its thick walls and majestic towers, was a symbol of the endurance and faith of the Templars. Under the benevolent protection of King Denis, the fortress came alive again, not with the clash of weapons, but with the murmur of prayers and the rustling of the monk-soldiers' robes.

The Creation of the Order of Christ.

To legitimize the presence of the Templars in Portugal and protect their interests against papal pressures, Denis I had an ingenious idea: the transformation of the order. In 1319, with the approval of Pope John XXII, he founded the Order of Christ. This new entity, spiritual and material heir of the Templars, allowed the knights to continue their mission under a different banner. The lands, goods and Templar fortresses, including Tomar, were transferred to the Order of Christ.

The Order of Christ preserved the chivalrous traditions of the Templars while adopting a more national and less international orientation. The knights continued to protect the routes of the pilgrims, to defend the Christian borders, and to participate in military campaigns against the Moors. Under the direction of the Order of Christ, Tomar became a centre of knowledge and devotion, a place where the legacy of the Templars was preserved and honoured.

Scotland: Land of Freedom and Resistance.

While Portugal offered an organized and structured refuge to the Templars, Scotland, with its steep mountains and misty valleys, became a more secret and elusive sanctuary. Far from the European power centres, Scotland was a land of resistance and freedom, where the authority of Philip IV and the papacy had little hold.

Robert the Bruce, king of Scotland, was then fighting for the independence of his kingdom against England. The Templars, with their military experience and dedication, found in him a natural ally. Bruce, appreciative of the help the Templars could bring to his cause, welcomed them with cautious but benevolent hospitality.

The Legends of Bannockburn.

One of the most enduring legends surrounding the flight of the Templars to Scotland is their participation in the Battle of Bannockburn in 1314. This decisive battle, where the Scots inflicted a crushing defeat on the English, is often shrouded in mystery and myths. According to some accounts, a group of knights in white armour, bearing red crosses, appeared on the battlefield, turning the tide of the confrontation in favour of the Scots.

Although the historical evidence of this participation is slim, the legend persists, fuelled by the mystery and fascination for the Templars. These knights, symbols of resistance and justice, would have found in the struggle for Scottish independence a cause worthy of their devotion.

The Templars and the Masons.

Another legend that links the Templars to Scotland is that of their connection with Freemasonry. Some historians and myths suggest that the Templars, fleeing after their persecution, would have found refuge among the guilds of masons and builders in Scotland. These guilds, rich in symbols and rituals, would have been influenced by Templar traditions, giving birth to modern Freemasonry.

The Templars are said to have passed on their secrets and esoteric knowledge to the masons, thus creating a spiritual and initiatory lineage that still persists today. The Scottish Masonic lodges, with their complex rituals and mysterious symbols, still bear the traces of this Templar influence.

The Hidden Life of the Templars in Scotland.

In Scotland, the Templars led a discreet life, often hidden from prying eyes. They settled in remote areas, blending in with the local population. Some became farmers, craftsmen or traders, while maintaining their secret identity as Knights Templar.

The Scottish Templars continued to practice their rites in secret, preserving their traditions and faith despite the dangers. The hidden chapels and places of worship became sanctuaries of their spiritual heritage. Among these places, Rosslyn Chapel, built by the St. Clair family, is often cited as a site of Templar tradition, rich in symbols and legends.

The Templars' Legacy.

The legacy of the Templars in Portugal and Scotland still endures today. In Tomar, the fortress and the convent of the Order of Christ remain as monuments to the memory of the knights, testifying to their resilience and adaptation. The castle of Tomar, with its majestic architecture and detailed frescoes, is a symbol of the Templar endurance and the continuity of their mission in a new form.

In Scotland, the shadow of the Templars still looms over the hills and valleys. Stories of mysterious knights, hidden treasures, and Masonic connections continue to fuel the collective imagination. The Scottish Templars, although less visible than their Portuguese counterparts, have left an indelible mark on local culture and traditions.

The Suspicions of Templar Presence in America.

Under the veil of mysteries and legends, the Templars continue to captivate the collective imagination. Among the many enigmas surrounding this chivalrous order, one of the most fascinating is their possible presence in America before the explorations of Christopher Columbus. Although concrete evidence is lacking, the stories, clues, and theories abound, weaving a tapestry of speculation and fascination.

The First Suspicions.

The first suspicions of Templar presence in America date back to stories and oral traditions passed down through the centuries. Some explorers and historians have suggested that the Templars, fleeing persecution in Europe after their arrest in 1307, may have sailed west, seeking refuge far from the influence of Philip IV and the papacy.

A popular theory suggests that the Templars, with their maritime expertise and powerful fleets, could have undertaken transatlantic voyages. Their advanced knowledge of navigation, inherited from their interactions with Mediterranean and Levantine civilizations, would have allowed them to brave the unknown waters of the Atlantic. Ancient maps, like the famous Piri Reis map, show surprising outlines of America, fuelling the idea that European explorers could have reached the New World long before Columbus.

The Archaeological Indices.

Among the clues often cited to support the Templar presence in America, several artifacts and mysterious structures arouse the interest of researchers and mystery enthusiasts. One of the most intriguing sites is the Newport Tower, in the state of Rhode Island in the United States. This stone structure, similar to European medieval towers, has fuelled speculation about a Templar origin.

Built with techniques reminiscent of those used by the Templars, the Newport Tower is often presented as potential evidence of their passage. Although some archaeologists attribute this tower to Nordic settlers or early European colonists, the possibility of an earlier construction by the Templars remains a subject of debate.

The Symbols and the Legends.

The Templar symbols, recognizable by their red crosses and distinctive architectural motifs, are sometimes invoked as evidence of their presence in America. Maltese crosses engraved in stone, knight motifs and other religious symbols have been reported in various locations, from the eastern United States to South America.

A notable example is the Westford stone, in Massachusetts, which bears an engraving in the shape of a knight with a sword and a shield. Some researchers see it as a tribute to a Templar knight, while others consider this engraving as a Native American artifact or a later colonial creation. The Westford stone, just like the Newport tower, continues to fuel discussions and hypotheses.

The Templars and the Order of Christ.

Another key element of the theory of the Templar presence in America is the Order of Christ, successor to the Templars in Portugal. The Order of Christ, under the direction of Infante Henry the Navigator, played a crucial role in the major Portuguese maritime explorations in the 15th century. Some historians suggest that the Order of Christ, inheritor of the Templar traditions and knowledge, may have continued the transatlantic voyages undertaken by their predecessors.

The Portuguese explorers, benefiting from the logistical and financial support of the Order of Christ, reached unknown territories, exploring the coasts of Africa and, eventually, the lands of America. The coat of arms of the Order of Christ, visible on the sails of Portuguese ships, recall the Templar iconography, reinforcing the idea of a continuity between the two orders and their role in the explorations.

The Manuscripts and the Testimonies.

Among the stories and written testimonies, some medieval manuscripts and navigation documents mention lands to the west of Europe, long before Columbus's voyage. Norwegian chronicles and Icelandic tales speak of distant lands, potentially linked to the legends of Vinland. Although these stories are often associated with the Vikings, some historians suggest that the Templars, in search of refuge, could have used this knowledge to explore the Atlantic.

Enigmatic manuscripts like the "Zeno Narrative" describe journeys to mysterious lands in the west, sometimes interpreted as pre-Columbian explorations. Although the authenticity of these documents is often contested, they add a fascinating dimension to the theory of the Templar presence in America.

Contemporary Theories.

Contemporary theories about the Templar presence in America continue to captivate researchers and writers. Works such as "Holy Blood, Holy Grail" and "The Templar Revelation" explore the links between the Templars, transatlantic explorations, and the mysteries of the New World. These theories, although controversial, have popularized the idea of a connection between the Knights Templar and the unknown lands of America.

Contemporary authors and researchers, by examining old maps, archaeological artifacts, and historical narratives, attempt to piece together a coherent picture of these hypothetical voyages. Although material evidence remains limited, the accumulated clues provide a basis for speculating on the motivations and means that would have driven the Templars to cross the Atlantic.

Conclusion: A Legend that Persists.

The Templar presence in America, although remaining a controversial theory, continues to exert a lasting fascination. The Templars, through their mystery and tragedy, embody the archetype of explorers and keepers of ancient secrets. Their hypothetical voyages across the Atlantic, in search of new lands and refuges far from persecution, add an epic dimension to their legend.

Archaeological evidence, symbols, narratives, and contemporary theories weave into a complex tapestry of mystery and possibility. Although definitive confirmation of their presence in America remains elusive, the quest to uncover the truth continues to inspire researchers and history enthusiasts.

The Templars, in their quest for refuge and renewal, remind us that the spirit of exploration and discovery transcends time. Their legend, fuelled by enigma and the aspiration to the unknown, remains a testament to the human quest for freedom, knowledge, and adventure.

The Treasure of the Templars: The Different Theories.

Beneath the thick shadows of fortresses and the secret vaults of Templar chapels, a mystery has persisted for centuries: that of the Templar treasure. Legendary, fascinating, this treasure symbolizes both the material wealth and the esoteric knowledge that the Knights Templar would have accumulated over the course of the crusades and their secret missions. Rumours and theories abound about what this treasure contained and where it might be hidden, igniting the collective imagination through the ages.

The Disappearance of the Treasure.

On October 13, 1307, when Philip IV of France ordered the mass arrest of the Templars, one of the main motivations was to seize their immense wealth. However, to the king's surprise and frustration, the much-coveted treasure had mysteriously disappeared. According to some chronicles, the Templars had been warned of the imminent arrest and had time to hide or move their treasure.

This disappearance gave rise to endless legends and speculations. Where had the Templars hidden their treasure? What riches and secrets did it contain? The answers to these questions are lost in the labyrinth of hypotheses and theories.

Theories on the Nature of the Treasure.

The descriptions of the Templars' treasure vary widely depending on the sources and theories. For some, it was material wealth: gold, silver, jewellery and precious artifacts accumulated during the Crusades. Others believe that the treasure included sacred relics and objects of great spiritual value, such as the Holy Grail, the Ark of the Covenant, or fragments of the True Cross.

There are also more esoteric theories suggesting that the real treasure of the Templars was not material but consisted of secret knowledge. Ancient manuscripts, alchemical texts, mysterious maps or secrets about the origins of Christianity could have been at the heart of this treasure. This hypothesis reinforces the mystical aura of the Templars, guardians of forbidden knowledge and deep mysteries.

The Likely Hideouts.

The Temple of Paris.

One of the most popular theories suggests that the Templars' treasure was hidden in their headquarters in Paris, known as the Paris Temple. This imposing fortress was the nerve centre of the order in France and housed their most valuable riches and documents.

However, during the arrest of the Templars, Philippe IV only found modest wealth compared to what he had hoped for. Some believe that the Templars had time to transfer their treasure elsewhere, leaving behind false trails to divert attention.

The Castle of Gisors.

The Château de Gisors, in Normandy, is another location often associated with the Templar treasure. This medieval castle, with its underground passages and secret hiding places, has long been surrounded by legends. Archaeological excavations have been carried out there over the years, some claiming to have found evidence of Templar presence.

In 1946, Abbot Mermet, a dowser, claimed to have located the treasure in the castle's underground tunnels. Although his claims have never been proven, they have fuelled the fascination for this place and its potential secrets.

Scotland and Rosslyn Chapel.

Scotland, land of mysteries and legends, is also cited as a possible hiding place for the Templar treasure. The Rosslyn Chapel, famous for its enigmatic sculptures and mysterious symbols, is often at the heart of these theories. Built in the 15th century by the St. Clair family, this chapel is supposed to house hidden Templar secrets in its foundations and ornaments.

The symbols present at Rosslyn Chapel, including representations of plants and unusual patterns for the time, have led some researchers to suggest that the Templars had brought knowledge and treasures to Scotland, far from the influence of the King of France.

Oak Island.

Oak Island, off the coast of Nova Scotia in Canada, is another site often mentioned in the legends of the Templar treasure. This mysterious island is famous for its "Money Pit", a complex excavation pit discovered in the 18th century. Explorations and excavations on the island have revealed artifacts and structures that could suggest sophisticated human activity long before the colonial era.

Some theorists suggest that the Templars, fleeing after their arrest in Europe, could have crossed the Atlantic and hidden their treasure on this isolated island. Although this theory is often criticized and considered speculative, it continues to captivate researchers and enthusiasts of lost treasures.

The Spiritual Treasure and the Secret Manuscripts.

Beyond material wealth, a persistent theory is that the true treasure of the Templars resided in their secret knowledge and manuscripts. Ancient documents and esoteric texts, including revelations about the origins of Christianity, alchemical secrets and occult knowledge, would have been hidden by the Templars to prevent them from falling into the wrong hands.

These manuscripts could have been hidden in secret libraries, isolated monasteries, or even transported to safe places beyond Europe. The quest for these documents continues to attract truth seekers, convinced that these writings contain knowledge capable of changing our understanding of history and spirituality.

The Unfathomable Mysteries.

Despite the numerous theories and intensive research, the mystery of the Templars' treasure remains unfathomable. The disappearance of their wealth and the persistence of legends fuel the collective imagination and feed stories of quest and discovery.

Each generation of researchers and adventurers hopes to be the one to finally unlock the secret of the Templars, but the treasure remains elusive, hidden in the mists of time and the corners of history. Perhaps the true treasure of the Templars is precisely this endless quest, a symbol of the perpetual search for truth, justice, and knowledge.

The Templar Artifacts discovered by Hamilton White and Carl Cookson.

The recent discoveries of two enthusiasts, Hamilton White and Carl Cookson, have rekindled interest in the treasures and secrets of the Knights Templar. Their quest, both archaeological and spiritual, has unearthed a collection of Templar artifacts of exceptional importance, illuminating new facets of this enigmatic and fascinating order.

Hamilton White began buying and selling antiques, artifacts, and collectibles from his adolescence, which allowed him to amass a considerable fortune. His personal collection includes historical artifacts of impressive proportions, ranging from prehistoric to medieval, including historical weapons. His home surpasses most museums in terms of wealth and diversity of the collection.

Carl Cookson, for his part, made a fortune in real estate. Passionate about cars and motorcycles, he owns an impressive collection of vehicles. Their friendship began when they both lived in Monaco. Cookson owned an old Templar property and, upon learning this, White, whose interest in the history of the Templars had existed for many years, visited the property. This encounter led to a collaboration to search for objects known as the Treasure of Tomar.

The Treasure of Tomar is a collection of weapons, helmets, and chalices believed to have belonged to the Templars, famous for their exploits during the Crusades between the 12th and 14th centuries. Hamilton White spent years gathering the scattered pieces since the initial discovery in 1960 in Tomar, Portugal, a site of a significant Templar fortress.

Among the notable items in their collection, there is a sword potentially worn by a Grand Master Templar who died at the siege of Acre in 1291, a spectacular obsidian chalice made from one of the rarest materials in the world, a medieval marble libation cup, and an ornate reliquary box, likely made in the early 13th century. This box, measuring 29 cm high, is decorated with several figures, possibly Saint George and Jesus Christ in monk's robes.

Their collection is not limited to these artifacts. It also includes sacred relics, such as fragments of the True Cross and bones of saints, revered by the Templars for their spiritual power and divine protection. A beautifully ornate gold reliquary, containing a fragment of the True Cross, symbolizes the deep faith of the Templars and their dedication to the protection of holy places. The delicate details of the ornamentation recall the importance of these relics in the spiritual life of the knights.

Hamilton White and Carl Cookson have dedicated a significant part of their lives to the research and preservation of these historical objects. Their passion for history and their ability to acquire rare artifacts has resulted in a collection that offers unique insights into the life and beliefs of the Templars.

Conclusion: A Journey Through Time.

The Templar artifacts discovered by Hamilton White and Carl Cookson are not just ancient objects; they are the guardians of the history and mysteries of the Knights Templar. Each piece of their collection, carefully preserved and studied, offers a valuable insight into the life and beliefs of this legendary order.

Through these discoveries, the past of the Templars comes back to life, illuminating the dark corners of history with flashes of bravery, faith, and mysticism. White and Cookson's quest, far more than a simple treasure hunt, is a journey through time, an exploration of the depths of Templar history, and a celebration of the enduring legacy of the Knights Templar.

Chapter 7: The Legacy of the Templars.

Influence on Subsequent Military Orders.

Under the starry sky of medieval history, the Templars, these monk-soldiers with white cloaks adorned with red crosses, have left an indelible mark. Their order, founded at the beginning of the 12th century to protect pilgrims in the Holy Land, quickly became a model of discipline, bravery, and dedication. Although their end was tragic, their influence continued to be felt through the centuries, inspiring and shaping subsequent military orders.

The Spiritual and Military Legacy of the Templars.

The Templars, with their unique blend of monastic and military life, established a model that other orders followed. Their rule, written by Bernard of Clairvaux, and their hierarchical structure, based on discipline and obedience, laid the foundations for the military orders that followed them. Their commitment to the vows of poverty, chastity, and obedience, combined with their mission of protection and holy war, became a standard for religious military orders.

The Hospitallers of Saint John of Jerusalem.

The Order of the Hospitallers, founded before the Templars, found in them a model and a rival. After the dissolution of the Templars, the Hospitallers received a large part of their assets, but it was their structure and discipline that they integrated most deeply. The Hospitallers, while continuing their mission of caring for sick and injured pilgrims, adopted aspects of the Templar organization to strengthen their military capacity.

The Hospitallers, later known as the Knights of Rhodes and finally of Malta, combined the charitable and military aspects of the Templars, becoming one of the most powerful military orders in the Mediterranean. Their fleet and fortresses became bastions against Muslim incursions, perpetuating the Templars' legacy of protection and holy war.

The Teutonic Order.

The Teutonic Order, founded at the end of the 12th century, was strongly influenced by the Templars. This German order, created to assist pilgrims in the Holy Land and protect the Crusader states, quickly adopted the Templar model of monk-soldiers. Their rule, inspired by that of the Templars, combined monastic life with military duty.

After the fall of the Crusader States, the Teutonic Order turned to Eastern Europe, where they led crusades against the Baltic pagans. They established a monastic state in Prussia, structured in a military and administrative manner, with powerful fortresses and strict discipline, reminiscent of the Templar traditions. Their conquests and military governance consolidated their power and influence in the region, perpetuating the legacy of the Templars in a new geographical and political context.

The Order of Calatrava.

In Spain, the Order of Calatrava, founded in the 12th century, was another military order that learned from the Templars. Tasked with defending the Christian borders against the Moors, the knights of Calatrava adopted the Cistercian rule and an austere way of life similar to that of the Templars. Their military organization and their commitment to the Reconquista reflected the influence of the Temple's monk-soldiers.

The Order of Calatrava, along with other Spanish military orders such as the Orders of Santiago and Alcántara, played a crucial role in the Reconquista, using military strategies and discipline inspired by the Templars to repel Muslim forces and reconquer Spanish lands.

The Knights of the Order of Christ.

In Portugal, the Order of Christ, founded in 1319 after the dissolution of the Templars, was directly derived from the Templar heritage. Denis I, king of Portugal, transformed the Portuguese Templars into Knights of the Order of Christ, thus preserving their traditions and mission in a new form. The Order of Christ played a crucial role in Portugal's major maritime explorations, providing logistical and spiritual support to explorers like Vasco de Gama and Ferdinand Magellan.

The symbols and traditions of the Templars were integrated into the Order of Christ, perpetuating their legacy through the age of discoveries. The Portuguese caravels, bearing the cross of the Order of Christ, carried within them the spirit of adventure and faith of the Templars, sailing towards unknown worlds with the same dedication and determination as their predecessors.

The Orders of Saint Lazarus and Saint Mary of Jerusalem.

The Orders of Saint Lazarus and Saint Mary of Jerusalem, although less known, were also influenced by the Templars. The Order of Saint Lazarus, initially dedicated to the care of lepers, adopted military aspects in response to the defence needs of the Crusader states. The Order of Saint Mary of Jerusalem, founded in Germany, followed a similar evolution, combining charity with a military mission.

These orders, while maintaining their charitable missions, incorporated elements of military discipline and organizational structure from the Templars, demonstrating the lasting influence of the latter on the design of religious and military orders.

The Moral and Spiritual Heritage.

Beyond the organization and structure, the moral and spiritual legacy of the Templars continued to influence subsequent military orders. Their commitment to the defence of the Christian faith, their devotion to monastic vows, and their ideal of pure chivalry became standards for knights in the following centuries.

The Templars embodied an ideal of bravery, sacrifice, and unwavering faith. Their example inspired not only military orders, but also chivalric culture in general. Templar values, passed down through the centuries, nourished legends and heroic tales, reinforcing the image of the knight devoted to the protection of the weak and the fight against injustice.

Legends and Myths around the Templars.

In the depths of medieval history, where reality and myth blend, the Templars remain enigmatic figures, surrounded by mysteries and legends. From their creation in the early 12th century to their abrupt dissolution in the early 14th century, the Templars have captivated the collective imagination, generating fascinating stories that continue to haunt minds and inspire storytellers.

The Holy Grail and the Sacred Relics.

Among the most famous legends surrounding the Templars, that of the Holy Grail stands out for its power of fascination. The Holy Grail, this sacred cup supposed to have collected the blood of Christ, is often associated with the Templars in popular stories. According to some legends, the Templars would have discovered the Grail during their excavations under the Temple of Jerusalem and would have kept it secret, protecting it with sacred zeal.

The tales tell that the Grail conferred extraordinary powers and infinite wisdom to those who possessed it. The Templars, as guardians of this divine treasure, were supposed to have acquired esoteric knowledge and mystical powers, distinguishing them from other religious orders. The quest for the Grail, immortalized by writers such as Chrétien de Troyes and Wolfram von Eschenbach, became a symbol of the ultimate spiritual quest, and the Templars were its enigmatic protagonists.

The Ark of the Covenant and the Mysteries of the Temple.

Another persistent legend associates the Templars with the Ark of the Covenant, this sacred artifact of the Hebrews that contained the tablets of the Law given to Moses. According to some accounts, the Templars would have discovered the Ark under the Temple of Jerusalem and brought it back to Europe. This legend fuels speculation about the nature of the treasures hidden by the Templars and the secrets they would have taken with them.

Rumours about the Templar excavations under the Temple of Jerusalem add an additional layer of mystery. It is said that the Templars found ancient documents and sacred relics there, uncovering forbidden knowledge and age-old secrets. These discoveries would have strengthened their power and influence, giving them an aura of mysticism and hidden knowledge.

The Templars and Freemasonry.

One of the most persistent legends links the Templars to Freemasonry. According to this theory, the Templars, after their dissolution in 1307, would have taken refuge among the guilds of masons and builders, transmitting their secrets and traditions. These guilds would then have evolved to become modern Freemasonry, inheriting the symbols and rituals of the Templars.

The Masonic lodges, with their complex rituals and mysterious symbols, would thus be the custodians of the Templar traditions. The Masonic degrees, symbolic tools, and initiatory ceremonies evoke the secret practices of the Templars, suggesting a spiritual and philosophical continuity between the two orders. This legend feeds the collective imagination, linking the Templars to an influential and mysterious secret society.

The Curse of Jacques de Molay.

The tragic end of the Templars, marked by the arrest and execution of their leaders, gave birth to a legend of revenge and curse. Jacques de Molay, the last grand master of the Templars, is said to have, according to legend, cursed King Philip IV and Pope Clement V from his pyre. He is said to have summoned them before the court of God, prophesying their imminent death.

This curse, reported by contemporaries and taken up by chroniclers, seems to have had a sinister echo in the months that followed. Philip IV died in 1314, shortly after the execution of Jacques de Molay, closely followed by Pope Clement V. The sudden deaths of these powerful figures were perceived as the fulfilment of the grand master's curse, reinforcing the mystical and formidable aura of the Templars.

The Hidden Treasures and Mysterious Hideouts.

The mystery of the Templar treasures is another inexhaustible source of legends. It is said that the Templars, warned of their imminent arrest, hid their treasures in secret places across Europe. From the mountains of Scotland to the castles of France and the islands of Portugal, the supposed hiding places of the Templar treasures fuel dreams of fortune and adventure.

The treasure of Oak Island, off the coast of Nova Scotia, is one of the most famous sites associated with the Templar treasures. Excavations have revealed complex structures and mysterious artifacts, suggesting a sophisticated human presence long before the colonial era. Treasure hunters, convinced that the Templars hid their wealth there, continue to dig and explore, hoping to discover priceless treasures.

Ghostly Apparitions and Haunted Places.

The legends surrounding the Templars also include tales of ghosts and haunted places. The ruins of the Templar commanderies, the ancient fortresses and castles associated with the order are often considered sites where one can encounter spectral apparitions. The ghosts of knights in armour, standing guard in the shadow of the old stones, haunt popular stories.

These apparitions, perceived as the souls of the Templars unjustly accused and executed, add a supernatural dimension to their legend. Visitors to the old commanderies report sensations of cold, incomprehensible whispers, and fleeting visions, reinforcing the idea that the Templars continue to watch over their secrets and treasures, even after death.

The Templars and the Alchemical Secrets.

Another fascinating legend associates the Templars with alchemy and the quest for the philosopher's stone. According to some theories, the Templars would have discovered alchemical secrets during their travels in the East, including knowledge about the transmutation of metals and the elixir of long life. These secrets, transmitted through hidden manuscripts, would have allowed the order to accumulate extraordinary wealth and power.

The alchemical symbols, present in certain Templar artifacts and manuscripts, feed this legend. The Templars, guardians of hermetic secrets, would have become master alchemists, pursuing spiritual and material quests beyond the simple protection of pilgrims and holy places.

Conclusion: A Legacy of Mysteries.

The legends and myths surrounding the Templars weave a complex tapestry of mysticism, bravery, and mystery. These stories, although often embellished and romanticized, reflect the profound impact of the order on the collective imagination. The Templars, both heroes and martyrs, guardians of treasures and secrets, continue to captivate minds and inspire stories of adventure, quest, and discovery.

Beyond historical facts, the legends of the Templars remind us of the importance of spiritual quest and the search for truth. They invite us to explore the mysteries of our own existence, to seek light in the darkness, and to discover the hidden treasures of our soul.

Chapter 8: Timeline of Major Events.

Foundation and Ascension (1118-1147).

In the year 1118, amidst the tumult and fervour of the Crusades, the Order of the Templars was born. Nine French knights, among them Hugues de Payens and Geoffroy de Saint-Omer, banded together to protect pilgrims in the Holy Land. They took vows of poverty, chastity, and obedience, drawing from the principles of monastic life while embracing the role of holy warriors.

The Order received official recognition in 1129, when the Council of Troyes, under the impetus of Bernard of Clairvaux, approved their rule of life. Bernard, eloquent and charismatic, praised their cause and their dedication, attracting many knights and wealthy donations. Quickly, the Templars rose in power, building fortresses and commanderies across Europe and the Middle East.

Expansion and Power (1147-1291).

During the Second Crusade (1147-1149), the Templars demonstrated their military value, supporting the Christian armies and playing a crucial role in the defence of the conquered territories. Their reputation for discipline and bravery only grew, and with it, their political and economic influence.

Their presence extended, from the fertile lands of Western Europe to the burning sands of the Holy Land. The Templars became bankers and advisors, administrators of vast estates and protectors of trade routes. Their growing power aroused respect and admiration, but also envy and suspicion.

In 1187, after the crushing defeat at Hattin against Saladin, the Templars lost Jerusalem. However, their determination remained intact, and they continued to fight, playing a crucial role in the efforts to retake the Holy Land.

In 1291, the fall of Acre marked the end of the Latin states in the East. The Templars, desperate, were forced to leave the Holy Land, but their influence in Europe remained strong.

Decline and Betrayal (1307-1314).

On Friday, October 13, 1307, a thunderclap resounded throughout Christendom: Philip IV of France, nicknamed Philip the Fair, ordered the arrest of all the Templars in his kingdom. Accused of heresy, blasphemy, and obscene practices, the knights were imprisoned, tortured, and forced to confess imaginary crimes.

The confessions, obtained under torture, were used to legitimize the actions of the king and to confiscate the immense wealth of the Order. Pope Clement V, under pressure from the king of France, convened a council to examine the accusations. In 1312, the order of the Templars was officially dissolved by the papal bull "Vox in excelso". The assets of the Templars were largely transferred to the Hospitallers, but the best parts were seized by Philip IV.

On March 18, 1314, Jacques de Molay, the last grand master of the Templars, and Geoffroy de Charnay, preceptor of Normandy, were burned alive at the stake in Paris. According to legend, Jacques de Molay, in his last words, cursed Philip IV and Clement V, summoning them before God's tribunal before the end of the year. Strangely, both men died shortly after, adding an aura of mystery and divine vengeance to the tragic end of the Templars.

Heritage and Legends (1314-present).

Despite their official disappearance, the Templars left a lasting legacy. Their influence was felt through the military orders that succeeded them, such as the Hospitallers and the Teutonic Knights, who adopted and adapted the Templar structures and ideals.

Legends about hidden treasures, sacred relics, and the secret knowledge of the Templars thrived. Theories linking the Templars to

Freemasonry emerged, suggesting that the order had passed on its secrets and traditions through secret societies. These legends were fuelled by popular stories and literary works, immortalizing the Templars as guardians of mysteries and occult knowledge.

Two Centuries of Holy Wars.

Thus concludes the epic of the holy wars which, for two centuries, had drawn all the forces of Christian Europe to the East. During this tumultuous period, the sword of the Templar knights never had a respite. The knights, driven by immense courage but often lacking adequate military experience, found themselves continually besieged by numerous and relentless enemies.

The Templars, faced with desperate circumstances, proved tireless in their defence. Their bravery, dedication, and sacrifice were constant. By examining the fate of the grand masters, almost all perishing in battle or from their wounds, one better understands the extent of their commitment. These leaders, falling with weapons in hand, embodied the spirit of sacrifice that animated the order.

The esteem and admiration that these warriors inspired were immense, particularly in an era where military glory was revered. The Christian world resounded with their exploits, and princes and sovereigns sought the honour of wearing the order's habit or dying in it.

The history of the Templars in Palestine reflects their greatness and their rise to a peak of glory. However, the fall of Acre marked the beginning of an inevitable period of decline. The glory days were numbered, and the order would soon face even more terrible trials.

Pivotal Dates in the History of the Templars.

1118: Foundation of the Order of the Templars by Hugues de Payens and eight other knights in Jerusalem.

1129: Official recognition of the Order at the Council of Troyes, supported by Bernard de Clairvaux.

1147-1149: Notable participation of the Templars in the Second Crusade, strengthening their military reputation.

1187: Defeat of the Christians at the Battle of Hattin and loss of Jerusalem to Saladin.

1291: Fall of Acre, marking the end of the Crusader states in the Holy Land and the withdrawal of the Templars to Europe.

1307: Massive arrest of the Templars in France on the order of Philippe IV, Friday, October 13th.

1312: Dissolution of the Order by Pope Clement V through the bull "Vox in excelso".

1314: Execution of Jacques de Molay and Geoffroy de Charnay in Paris, marking the official end of the Order.

Chapter 9: Chronology of the Grand Masters of the Templars.

I. Hugues de Payens (de Paganis) 1118 – 1136.

Hugues de Payens, this name resonates like a legend in medieval epics. Founder and first grand-master of the Order of the Templars, his story is that of a man whose courage and devotion would forever change the course of Christian history in the Holy Land. Born into a noble family in Champagne, Hugues de Payens is an emblematic figure who embodies the chivalrous and religious values of his time. His life, marked by loss and despair, transformed into a sacred quest that would establish a military order of unparalleled influence.

André Duschesne, renowned historian, reports that Hugues de Payens was driven to Palestine by the despair of having lost his fiancée, Jourelaine de Cabanais and de Cofolant. This personal tragedy, far from plunging him into oblivion, pushed him to embrace a cause greater than himself. The pain of loss transformed into an unwavering devotion to the defence of the Christian faith. In Palestine, he found a new purpose in his life by dedicating himself to the protection of pilgrims and holy places.

In 1118, Hugues de Payens, along with eight other French knights, founded the order of the Templars. Their mission: to protect pilgrims on their way to Jerusalem from the dangers that lurked on the perilous paths of the Holy Land. The king of Jerusalem, Baldwin II, gave them a house near the Temple of Solomon, from which they got the name "Templars". From then on, their order distinguished itself by a strict observance of the three religious vows: chastity, obedience and poverty, but also by a rigorous military discipline.

Hugues de Payens, as the first grand master, played a crucial role in the organization and expansion of the order. In 1128, he went to Europe to solicit the support of nobles and kings. He participated in the Council of Troyes, where the order received official recognition and a rule, written by Saint Bernard of Clairvaux, one of the most influential men of the time. This rule combined elements of monastic life and military discipline, making the Templars a unique and formidable force.

Under the leadership of Hugues de Payens, the Templars experienced rapid growth. Chapters were established in several regions of Europe, receiving donations of land, castles, and other goods. The order became not only a military power, but also a prosperous economic institution. Their presence in the Holy Land strengthened, and they played a crucial role in battles and sieges, defending Christian territories against Muslim incursions.

Hugues de Payens died in 1136, mourned by all zealous Christians in Palestine. His death marked the end of a founding and initial expansion era for the Templars. His leadership and vision had laid the solid foundations of an order that would endure for nearly two centuries. The Templars, under his direction, had gained not only in military strength but also in respect and influence within the Christian world.

The year of his death coincided, according to D. Vayssette, with the establishment of the oldest house of the order in Languedoc, founded in a place called La Nougarede, later known as Ville-dieu, in the county of Foix, by Count Roger III. This event underscores the continuous expansion of the order even after the disappearance of its founder. The Templars had managed to establish strong bastions not only in the Holy Land but also in Europe, thus ensuring the continuity and stability of their mission.

The legacy of Hugues de Payens was not limited to his military accomplishments. He also left an indelible mark on the ideology and structure of chivalric orders. His ability to combine spirituality and war, to create a body of knights dedicated not only to battle but also to the protection of Christian values, was revolutionary. This model inspired not only the Templars but also other military orders that followed.

The influence of Hugues de Payens extended well beyond his time. The principles he established continued to guide the Templars for generations. The order became a pillar of Christian defence in the Holy

Land, playing key roles in subsequent crusades. Their fortress, their discipline, and their dedication made them both respected and feared figures.

The life of Hugues de Payens is a testament to the impact an individual can have on the course of history. Transforming his personal pain into a noble cause, he created an institution that changed the landscape of his time. His legacy endures, not only in historical accounts but also in the collective imagination, where the Templars continue to symbolize courage, faith, and sacrifice.

Today, the name of Hugues de Payens is associated with a period of religious fervour and conflict, but also of transformation and innovation. He embodies the spirit of the Crusades, with all its contradictions and passions. By founding the Templars, he opened a new path for knights, a path where spirituality and combat converged to defend a greater ideal.

In conclusion, Hugues de Payens, through his leadership and vision, left an indelible mark on the history of the Templars and the Crusades. His life, marked by mourning and the quest for justice, transformed into a legend of heroism and dedication. The values he promoted, the organization he put in place, and the example he set continued to inspire long after his death, making him a central figure in Christian medieval history.

II. Robert de Craon, known as the Burgundian (1136-1147).

The name of Robert de Craon, often called the Burgundian, evokes a prominent figure of the Order of the Templars. Third son of Renaud II, lord of Craon, Robert succeeded Hugues de Payens as grand master of the Temple in 1136. His journey, marked by the nobility of his origins and the fervour of his devotion, embodies the chivalrous and religious spirit of his time. Husband of Richeza, the only sister of Saint Anselm, Robert abandoned his wife in 1107 to devote himself to the sacred cause in the Holy Land, a decision that would lead him to memorable adventures and significant challenges.

Upon his accession to the magisterium of the Temple, Robert de Craon faced numerous trials. In 1139, the Knights Templar, allied with the French army, undertook a bold campaign towards Lisbon. Mounted on 70 ships, they laid siege to the city, hoping for a resounding victory. However, this venture ended in a crushing defeat and the knights were routed. This episode revealed the immense challenges that the Templars had to overcome, despite their bravery and determination.

The failure of Lisbon did not shake Robert de Craon's resolve. In 1146, he participated in a new expedition to Spain against the Moors, a campaign that would last ten years. The Knights Templar, alongside the Hospitallers, played a crucial role in this epic struggle. Their participation in this holy war demonstrated once again their dedication to the Christian cause and their military competence.

The year 1147 marked a turning point for the Templars under the leadership of Robert de Craon. The knights gathered in Paris to discuss matters of the Holy Land. This assembly was honoured by the presence of King Louis VII, known as Louis the Young. This solemn moment, although poorly documented, highlights the increasing importance of the Templars in the political and military affairs of the time.

The same year, Robert de Craon met his death, leaving behind a legacy of bravery and piety. William of Tyre, a chronicler of the time, attests that Robert was no less illustrious for the purity of his morals and his bravery than for the brilliance of his birth. His exemplary conduct and inspiring leadership allowed the Templars to overcome numerous challenges and continue their sacred mission.

Under the leadership of Robert de Craon, the Templars continued to consolidate their influence in the Holy Land and Europe. Their involvement in battles against the Moors in Spain attests to their active and decisive role in the conflicts of the time. The alliances forged with other military orders and royal support strengthened their position and their ability to conduct prolonged campaigns.

Robert de Craon's dedication to the cause of the Templars was not limited only to the battlefields. He also worked to strengthen the structure and organization of the order, laying the foundations for its future expansion. His leadership allowed the Templars to establish strict discipline and effective management of their resources, essential for maintaining their power and influence.

The death of Robert de Craon in 1147 marked the end of a period of challenges and achievements for the Templars. His successor inherited an order strengthened by Robert's efforts and dedication. The principles of moral purity and bravery that he embodied continued to guide the Templars in their future missions.

The legacy of Robert de Craon, although often overshadowed by that of his predecessor Hugues de Payens, remains significant. His unwavering commitment to the defence of the Christian faith and the protection of pilgrims in the Holy Land leaves a lasting imprint in the history of the Templars. His journey illustrates the fusion of chivalrous and religious ideals, characteristic of the era of the Crusades.

III. Evrard des Barres (1147-1149).

Evrard des Barres, an enigmatic and charismatic figure, was elected by the chapter of his order to succeed Robert de Craon, known as the Burgundian. An eminent Frenchman, he had already demonstrated his skills and devotion as a tutor or private master of the Templars in France since 1143. His rise to the rank of grand master testifies to the trust and respect he inspired within the order.

In 1148, as the Holy Land was once again plunged into chaos and war, Evrard des Barres led his knights to meet Louis VII, King of France, nicknamed Louis-the-Young. The latter had come to the aid of Christians in Palestine, but his army, weakened by successive defeats and harassed by the Turks in the formidable passes of Pamphylia, risked annihilation. Evrard, with the bravery and strategy that characterized the Templars, guided the royal army out of these imminent dangers, serving as their guide and protector to continue their journey to the Holy Land.

During the stay of Louis VII in Syria, the Templars, under the direction of Evrard des Barres, rendered him invaluable services. The letters that the king addressed to Suger, his minister, testify to the gratitude and admiration he felt for Evrard and his knights. In one of these missives, Evrard is explicitly named Grand Master of the Temple, an official recognition of his leadership and his crucial role in these military campaigns.

Evrard des Barres perfectly embodied the spirit of the Templar Order, combining military skills and religious devotion. His strategic ability saved the royal army from certain destruction, thus strengthening the position of the Templars in the Holy Land and their reputation in Europe. Thanks to him, the knights of the order continued to play a decisive role in the protection of pilgrims and in crucial battles against Muslim forces.

In 1149, as the situation in the Holy Land seemed to somewhat stabilize, Evrard accompanied Louis VII on his return to France. At Clairvaux, an emblematic place of Cistercian spirituality, Evrard made a surprising and radical choice: he embraced monastic life. Renouncing his responsibilities as grand master, he sent his abdication to Palestine, preferring the tranquillity and contemplation of monastic life to the glory and tumult of battles. Despite the pressing pleas of the Templars who begged him to return, Evrard remained firm in his decision, persevering in his new vocation.

Evrard des Barres' choice to retire to Clairvaux to lead a monastic life is indicative of the complexity and depth of his character. Although he was an accomplished military leader, capable of leading his men with bravery and strategy, he also felt an intense spiritual call, a longing to draw closer to God in quiet and prayer. This decision illustrates the Templar ideal of the fusion between the warrior and the monk, a delicate balance between action and contemplation.

The brief tenure of Evrard des Barres, although limited to only two years, had a lasting impact on the order of the Templars. His leadership during a period of crisis strengthened the position of the order and demonstrated the importance of the guidance and protection provided by the Templars to the crusaders in the Holy Land. His abdication, although surprising, did not diminish the respect and admiration his contemporaries had for him. On the contrary, it reinforced his image as a man of deep faith and conviction, ready to sacrifice earthly glory for a life of spiritual devotion.

The transition of Evrard des Barres from Grand Master to Cistercian monk also symbolizes the tensions and spiritual aspirations of the time. The Templars, while being formidable warriors, were also men of faith, dedicated to an ideal of divine service. Evrard's decision reminds us that even the greatest military leaders could be drawn to the peace and simplicity of monastic life, seeking to draw closer to God away from the battlefields.

Evrard des Barres' legacy is found not only in his military exploits but also in his example of spiritual life. By leaving the leadership of the order to embrace monastic life, he showed that true strength lies as much in faith and devotion as in bravery and strategy. His journey inspired many Templars and other knights, highlighting the importance of spirituality and contemplation in a life of service.

IV. Bernard de Tremelay (1149-1153).

Bernard de Tremelay, a knight of the highest nobility of Bugey, became Grand Master of the Templars at the end of the year 1149, succeeding Evrard des Barres. His appointment to the head of the order came at a time of great trials and challenges for Christians in the Holy Land. Bernard, with his bravery and dedication, embodied the chivalrous and religious values that were at the heart of the Templar order.

In 1150, Bernard de Tremelay led his knights under the orders of King Baldwin III to oppose the progress of Nur ad-Din, a prominent Muslim leader who threatened the crusader territories. Their campaign led them to the castle of Harenc, a strategic fortress. Despite their determination, they were forced to withdraw after several days of unsuccessful attack. This episode highlighted the increasing difficulties that the Templars and other crusaders were facing against increasingly organized and determined opponents.

In 1152, another threat loomed on the horizon. The Muslim forces had advanced to the Mount of Olives, a position of symbolic and strategic importance for Jerusalem. The knights of the two orders, the Templars and the Hospitallers, supported by the inhabitants of Jerusalem, managed to repel this advance. This act of bravery and determination once again highlighted the importance of the Templars in the defence of Christian territories in the Holy Land.

The following year, in 1153, Bernard de Tremelay and his knights participated in the siege of Ascalon, a key fortress on the Mediterranean coast. This siege, marked by intense fighting and fierce resistance from the Muslim defenders, severely tested the Christian forces. The Templars, true to their reputation for courage and tenacity, played a central role in the assaults on the city.

On August 12, 1153, after a long and difficult resistance, Ascalon finally capitulated. However, in their impatience and zeal to quickly enter the city through a random breach, the Templars suffered a terrible tragedy. About forty of them, including Bernard de Tremelay, were trapped by the Muslim defenders. They were all massacred, and Bernard, grand master of the order, was not spared. His head was severed like those of his companions, marking a tragic and heroic end to his career.

The death of Bernard de Tremelay was a heavy blow for the Templars and for all Christians in the Holy Land. His leadership, bravery, and exemplary dedication left a void that was difficult to fill. William of Tyre, the chronicler of the time, and other contemporary historians bear witness to his unwavering courage and commitment to the Christian cause.

Under the leadership of Bernard de Tremelay, the Templars continued to embody the ideals of the order: the defence of the Christian faith, the protection of pilgrims, and the fight against opposing forces. Although his tenure was brief, it marked a period of intense battles and heroic sacrifices.

The siege of Ascalon and the death of Bernard de Tremelay illustrate the relentless challenges the Templars faced. Their mission in the Holy Land was perilous, marked by bloody battles, prolonged sieges, and constant sacrifices. The bravery of the Templars, embodied by figures like Bernard de Tremelay, continued to inspire and galvanize Christian forces in their struggles against Muslim invaders.

The legacy of Bernard de Tremelay is that of a devoted knight and leader, whose life and death exemplify the ideals of the Templar order. His bravery, dedication, and sacrifice bear witness to the Templars' deep commitment to their sacred mission. By standing at the forefront of battles, guiding his knights with determination, and making the ultimate sacrifice for the Christian cause, Bernard de Tremelay left an indelible mark in the history of the Crusades.

V. Bertrand de Blanquefort (1153-1168).

Bertrand de Blanquefort, son of Godefroy, lord of Blanquefort in Guyenne, succeeded Bernard de Tremelay as Grand Master of the Knights Templar in 1153. Under his leadership, the order experienced moments of glory and trials, and Bertrand distinguished himself with his courage, military strategy and unwavering faith.

In 1156, the fate of Bertrand de Blanquefort took a dramatic turn. On June 19, he and eighty-seven of his knights were ambushed in a pass by the forces of Nur ad-Din, the Sultan of Syria, and were taken prisoner. This capture was a heavy blow for the Templars and for Christianity in the Holy Land. Emboldened by this success, Nur ad-Din continued his advance and laid siege to the castle of Panéas. However, the Templars, under the leadership of King Baldwin III, managed to lift the siege, demonstrating once again their resilience and determination.

Bertrand's captivity lasted three years. During this period, he demonstrated remarkable endurance and an indomitable spirit. In 1159, thanks to the efforts of the emperor of Constantinople, Bertrand and his companions regained their freedom. The negotiation led to the release of six thousand other captives, highlighting the importance of this exchange and the diplomatic influence of the Templars. This return was greeted with immense joy and boosted the morale of the crusaders in the Holy Land.

The liberation of Bertrand de Blanquefort marked a new phase in his leadership. Freed from the chains of captivity, he resumed the head of the Templars with renewed determination. His experiences as a prisoner enriched his wisdom and military strategy. He dedicated himself to strengthening the defences of Christian territories and consolidating the infrastructure of the order.

Bertrand de Blanquefort was not only a great military master, but also an edifying religious figure. His devotion to the Christian cause and his deep piety distinguished him among his peers. He was recognized for his integrity, wisdom and ability to inspire his knights. Under his magisterium, the order of the Templars strengthened its reputation for discipline, bravery and religious devotion.

During the magisterium of Bertrand, André de Montbard, maternal uncle of Saint Bernard of Clairvaux, played a crucial role within the order. André de Montbard, referred to as the master of the Temple by Abbot Geoffroy, was considered one of the strongest supporters of the Kingdom of Jerusalem. His influence and support were essential for the stability and strength of the order during this tumultuous period. The relationship between Bertrand and André de Montbard strengthened the spirit of the order, combining spiritual wisdom and military competence.

The following years were marked by constant confrontations and growing challenges. The Templars, under the leadership of Bertrand, continued to play a key role in the defence of Christian territories against Muslim incursions. Their strategic presence and their ability to mobilize resources were essential in maintaining a certain stability in the Holy Land.

In 1168, Bertrand de Blanquefort died, leaving behind a legacy of bravery, devotion, and wisdom. He was respected not only as a great military master, but also as a man of deep faith. His reputation as a pious man and accomplished captain endured well after his death.

Under his leadership, the Templars continued to embody the ideals of the order: the defence of pilgrims, the protection of holy places, and the fight against opposing forces. His exemplary leadership and sacrifices helped to strengthen the order and inspire future generations of knights.

The legacy of Bertrand de Blanquefort is that of a visionary leader who was able to guide the Templars through periods of crisis and challenge. His capture, release, and triumphant return not only illustrate his personal resilience but also the resilience of the Templar order. His unwavering devotion to the Christian cause and his commitment to protecting pilgrims and holy places remain powerful examples of leadership and faith.

VI. Philip of Nablus (1168-1174).

Philippe of Nablus, originally from the eponymous city in Syria, succeeded Bertrand de Blanquefort as Grand Master of the Templars in 1168. Born in Picardy, he was the eldest son of Gui de Milly and Stephanie, a Flemish lady. Before joining the order of the Templars, Philippe led a life marked by military commitments and lordly responsibilities.

Philippe had first been lord of Nablus and participated in the siege of Edessa in 1144, an emblematic battle that had profound repercussions on the Latin states of the East. Married and father of two daughters, the death of his wife pushed him to seek a new meaning in his life. His decision to become a Templar reflected a quest for devotion and service in a framework of rigorous faith and military discipline.

His commitment within the Templar Order was exemplary. Philippe quickly demonstrated leadership qualities and unwavering devotion, which earned him the position of Grand Master in 1168. His appointment to this high office is a testament to the respect and admiration he inspired among his peers. Philippe brought to the order not only his military experience, but also a deep understanding of the political and territorial issues of the Holy Land.

Under the leadership of Philippe of Nablus, the Templars continued to play a crucial role in the defence of Christian territories. His deep knowledge of the region and his past experience as lord of Nablus allowed him to lead effective strategies to protect pilgrims and holy places from Muslim incursions. However, his tenure was marked by constant challenges, both on the military and diplomatic fronts.

One of Philippe's main qualities was his ability to inspire and motivate his knights in times of crisis. His leadership during battles and sieges once again demonstrated the resilience and determination of the Templars. However, his time as Grand Master was relatively short, as he renounced this position before Easter of the year 1171. The precise reasons for this abdication remain unclear, but it is possible that they are related to the intense pressures and insurmountable challenges he was facing.

Philippe of Nablus's renunciation of his position as Grand Master did not diminish his legacy within the order. His tenure, although brief, was marked by exemplary devotion and impeccable conduct. The chronicles of the time, although succinct, pay tribute to his integrity and his ability to lead the order in periods of turbulence.

Philippe of Nablus embodies the spirit of the Templars, combining exceptional military skills with deep faith and a willingness to serve the Christian cause. His transition from lord to Templar, then to grand master, illustrates the quest for a higher ideal, characteristic of the knights of his time. His commitment to defending the holy places and protecting the pilgrims reflects the fundamental principles of the order of the Templars.

VII. Odon de Saint-Amand (1171-1179).

Odon de Saint-Amand, a French knight from a distinguished family, succeeded Philippe of Nablus as Grand Master of the Templars in 1171.

In 1172, at the beginning of his command, Odon de Saint-Amand had to face significant internal challenges. On one hand, with the apostasy of the Templar Mélier or Milon, brother of the Prince of Armenia. This defection had a profound impact on the order, testing the faith and cohesion of the knights. And on the other hand, shortly after, Gautier du Ménil, another knight of the Temple, massacred the deputy of the Prince of Assassins, leading to serious altercations. These internal incidents illustrate the tensions and difficulties that Odon had to face to maintain unity and discipline within the order.

The year 1177 was marked by the Battle of Ramlah against the forces of Saladin. Odon de Saint-Amand, leading eighty of his knights, actively participated in this confrontation. The Christians won the victory, but this success was short-lived. Saladin, determined and a formidable strategist, prepared his revenge and struck the following year.

While the Templars were building a fort near Panéas, Saladin attacked them again. King Baldwin IV, nicknamed Baldwin the Leper, flew to their rescue, but his efforts were in vain. The Franks were defeated, and Odon de Saint-Amand, along with several of his knights, were captured during the melee. The most distinguished knights were sent to Damascus, while the others were brutally executed on the battlefield.

Saladin proposed to Odon an exchange of his person for a captive emir of the Templars. Odon refused with a nobility that reflected the Templar ideal. "I do not want," he said, "to authorize by my example the cowardice of those of my religious who would let themselves be taken, with the view of being ransomed. A Templar must conquer or die, and can only give for his ransom his dagger or his belt." This statement of principle illustrated the determination of the Templars not to yield to weakness or compromise.

Odon de Saint-Amand died in captivity a few months later, in 1179. His refusal to be exchanged and his death in chains were a testament to his commitment and loyalty to the principles of the Templar order. The established custom among the Templars of not redeeming those who surrendered as prisoners and considering them as dead reinforced this ideology of bravery and ultimate sacrifice.

The period of Odon de Saint-Amand as Grand Master was brief but intense. It was marked by crucial military confrontations and significant internal challenges. His ability to maintain the cohesion of the order in the face of crises and to inspire his knights by his example of absolute dedication remains an essential part of the Templars' legacy.

Odon de Saint-Amand left a legacy of courage and loyalty. His death in captivity and his refusal to be exchanged demonstrated a deep understanding of duty and chivalrous honour. His example remained etched in the memory of his successors and all those who sought to understand the essence of the Templar commitment.

VIII. Alan or Arnaud de Toroge (1179-1184).

Alan de Toroge, also known as Arnaud de Toroge, ascended to the position of Grand Master of the Templars in 1179, succeeding Odon de Saint-Amand. Before his election, Alan had held several high positions within the order, demonstrating his skills and dedication to the Templar cause.

In 1180, a particularly challenging year for Christians in the Holy Land, Alan de Toroge and the Grand Master of the Hospitallers were forced to sign a dishonourable peace with Saladin. This truce, imposed by circumstances and the increasing military pressure from Muslim forces, reflected the strategic and political challenges that the military orders had to navigate. The signing of this peace, although necessary to avoid immediate defeat, was perceived as a humiliation and a setback for the efforts of the crusaders.

Despite this setback, Alan de Toroge never stopped looking for ways to strengthen the position of Christians in the Holy Land. In 1184, recognizing the need for more substantial support, Alan and the Grand Master of the Hospitallers embarked with Patriarch Heraclius on a mission to the West. Their goal was to solicit reinforcements and additional resources to continue the fight against Saladin's forces.

Their journey took them to the coasts of Italy, and they went to Verona, where Pope Lucius III was in conference with Emperor Frederick Barbarossa. This meeting was crucial, as it represented an opportunity for Christian leaders to strengthen their alliances and coordinate their efforts to support the Latin states of the East.

However, during this journey, Alan de Toroge fell seriously ill. Despite the care provided, he died in Verona in 1184, although some historians have wrongly claimed that he died in Paris. His death in foreign lands, far from the battlefields of the Holy Land, was a heavy blow for the Templars and for the mission they hoped to accomplish.

IX. Terric (Terricus) (1184-1188).

Terric, or Thierry, whose family origins and country of origin remain unknown, was elected Grand Master of the Templars after the death of Alan de Toroge in 1184.

In 1187, Terric, in concert with the Grand Master of the Hospital, launched a bold attack against Prince Afdhal, son of Saladin, on his return from a raid on the lands of the Franks. The balance of power was desperately unequal: five hundred Christians faced five thousand Muslims. Despite this disadvantage, the Templars and the Hospitallers fought with unparalleled courage, performing feats of bravery. The bravery of Jacquelin de Maillé was particularly noted, to the point that the Muslims took him for Saint George, the patron of Christian armies. However, almost all the knights perished in this heroic battle.

This confrontation took place on May 1, 1187. A few months later, on July 5, the famous Battle of Hattin took place near Tiberias, which lasted three days. The Templars, true to their reputation, were the first to descend into the plain and charged Saladin's troops with unparalleled determination. They initially repelled the enemy forces with admirable vigour and fearlessness, even surpassing their previous demonstrations of courage according to historians.

However, their bravery was betrayed by Raymond III, Count of Tripoli, who commanded the forces supposed to support the Templars. In an unthinkable betrayal, Raymond abandoned the Templars and fled, leaving his allies at the mercy of the enemy. Saladin, taking advantage of this betrayal, crushed the Christian forces. The Templars, isolated and outnumbered, were all killed or captured. The Battle of Hattin turned into a massacre, the Christian defeat being total and devastating.

Saladin offered the captured knights a chance of survival on the condition that they renounce their faith in Jesus Christ. The Templars, faithful to their vows and their faith, rejected this offer with horror and were all executed. Terric, the grand master, was the only one spared, but his capture marked the end of his ability to lead the Templars on the battlefield.

The defeat of Hattin was followed by the fall of all the strongholds in Syria and, tragically, of Jerusalem itself. In October 1187, Jerusalem, which had been under Christian control since its conquest by the first crusaders 88 years earlier, fell into the hands of Saladin. This loss marked one of the greatest tragedies of the Crusades era, symbolizing the collapse of Christian efforts in the Holy Land.

A few months after these events, Terric was released from his captivity. However, due to the oath he had made to Saladin to never take up arms against him, Terric felt obliged to resign from his position as grand master. Considering himself unable to continue governing the order under these restrictions, he withdrew, once again demonstrating the deep integrity and moral commitment that characterized the Templars.

The magisterium of Terric, although marked by defeats and devastating losses, was also a testament to the bravery and sacrifice of the Templars.

X. Gerard de Ridefort (1188-1189).

Gérard de Ridefort, also spelled de Ridefort or de Rédefort, belonged to a lineage of knights with roots in both Flanders and England. Succeeding Terric, Gérard took the reins of the Templar order at a time of upheaval and incessant conflict in the Holy Land.

His term was marked by intense battles and bold decisions. On October 4, 1189, Gerard de Ridefort commanded the reserve corps in the battle against Saladin. From the first clash, the enemy's right wing was overthrown, and victory initially seemed within reach for the Christian forces. However, the crusaders lacked discipline and, distracted by looting, lost the initiative. Saladin, an accomplished strategist, took advantage of this moment of weakness to counterattack with renewed vigour.

The situation could have turned into a massacre without the heroic resistance of the Templars. Gérard de Ridefort, true to his reputation for bravery, led his knights with unwavering determination. Their resistance helped to contain the enemy's advance, thus offering a chance for the Christian forces to regroup. However, this bravery came at a high cost. Gérard de Ridefort perished in action, accompanied by many Templars. According to a contemporary, his death was a glorious end to a series of remarkable feats.

However, the story of Gérard de Ridefort's death is subject to various interpretations. Corneille Zanfliel, a historian, places his death during the siege of Acre in 1191. This divergence in historical accounts underscores the uncertainties that sometimes surround the tumultuous events of this era.

After the death of Gérard de Ridefort, the position of Grand Master of the Templars remained vacant for eighteen months, a period of transition and uncertainty for the order. During this vacancy, a significant event marked the history of the Templars and the region. The King of England, Richard the Lionheart, took control of the island of Cyprus. To strengthen his campaign in the Holy Land, he pledged

Cyprus to the Templars for the considerable sum of twenty-five thousand silver marks. This financial commitment demonstrated the economic power and political influence of the order, even in times of crisis.

XI. Robert de Sablé (1191-1196).

Robert de Sablé, also spelled de Sabloil, was elected Grand Master of the Order of the Templars after the arrival of King Richard the Lionheart in Palestine. Commanding the fleet that had brought the King of England, Robert had become a Templar upon his arrival in front of Acre, impressing with his military exploits in Spain, Sicily and elsewhere. These achievements allowed him to bypass the usual probation periods, and he was quickly placed at the head of the Order of the Templars.

In 1191, barely admitted into the order, Robert de Sablé found himself plunged into the heart of the Third Crusade. Under his leadership and that of Richard the Lionheart, the Templars won a notable victory against Saladin in the plain of Arsuf in July of the same year. This victory, achieved thanks to the bravery and discipline of the Templars, secured the coastal route to Jaffa and was a crucial turning point in the efforts to retake Jerusalem.

Taking advantage of this victory, the Templars, with the help of the crusaders, undertook to repair and fortify the maritime strongholds, essential for maintaining supply and communication lines with Europe. Robert de Sablé's efforts in these fortification works were crucial in ensuring the stability and security of Christian territories in the Holy Land.

In 1192, a significant strategic decision was made by the Grand Master Robert de Sablé. Faced with difficulties in maintaining the island of Cyprus, a crucial territory recently acquired by Richard the Lionheart, Robert handed the island over to the King of England. This act demonstrated Robert's ability to make pragmatic decisions for the good of the order, even if it meant giving up a valuable territory.

However, not all of the Order's commitments under Robert de Sablé were crowned with success. In 1194, the Templars and the Hospitallers suffered a defeat in Spain against the Miramolin of Africa. This battle showed the constant challenges and multiple pressures to which the Order was subjected, not only in the Holy Land but also on other fronts.

The end of Robert de Sablé's magisterium approached quickly, and he died in 1196. Under his leadership, the Order of the Templars continued to play a central role in the Crusades, particularly during the Third Crusade led by Richard the Lionheart.

During or just before his magisterium, a new military order was born in Palestine: the order of the Teutonic Knights. This new order, intended to protect German pilgrims in the Holy Land, would survive and evolve to become a major force in northern Europe, long after the fall of the Latin states of the East.

XII. Gilbert Horal or Hérail (1196-1200).

Gilbert Horal, also known as Hérail, became Grand Master of the Knights Templar in 1196 after having been Preceptor of France. His tenure was marked by complex strategic decisions and internal conflicts that illustrate the challenges the Knights Templar faced at the end of the 12th century.

In 1197, a significant event marked the beginning of his leadership. The Templar Knights in Palestine refused to join their weapons with those of the imperials against the Muslims. This decision, motivated by honour and respect for oaths, was based on the truce concluded by King Richard the Lionheart with the enemy. The Templars had signed and sworn this truce, and they judged that it was against their duty to break this agreement. This refusal, although based on honorable principles, highlighted the tensions and strategic divergences between the different Christian factions in the Holy Land.

The year 1199 was marked by a major quarrel between the Templars and the Hospitallers, two of the most powerful military orders of the time. The rivalry, exacerbated by territorial disputes and conflicts of interest, degenerated into armed confrontations. To resolve this conflict, Terric, former grand master of the Temple, and Villeplane, one of his colleagues, were sent as delegates to Pope Innocent III.

The Pope, after severely reprimanding the two orders for their behaviour, referred the matter to the bishops of the East. These, after examination, condemned the Templars, accentuating the internal tensions within the order and between the military orders. This decision highlighted the administrative challenges and internal rivalries that could weaken the Christian cause in the Holy Land.

Despite these difficulties, Gilbert Horal sought to maintain the discipline and integrity of the Templar order. His management of the crisis and his efforts to preserve the values and commitments of the Templars testify to his determination to guide the order through tumultuous periods.

The year of Gilbert Horal's death is not precisely known, but he did not survive beyond the year 1201. His magisterium, although marked by internal conflicts and difficult strategic decisions, left a lasting imprint on the order of the Templars. His ability to navigate through moral dilemmas and internal rivalries shows the complexity of managing a military-religious order in times of war.

Gilbert Horal's leadership demonstrates the importance of integrity and commitment during times of conflict. His refusal to break the truce with the Muslims, despite pressures, shows a fidelity to the principles that guided the Templars through centuries of wars and crusades. The challenges he faced, both internal and external, testify to the resilience necessary to lead such an influential and complex order.

XIII. Philippe de Plessiez (1201-1217).

Philippe de Plessiez, born into a distinguished family from Anjou, ascended to the dignity of Grand Master of the Templars in 1201, according to the historian Ducange. His magisterium, spanning sixteen years, was marked by conflicts, political negotiations, and military exploits that strengthened the reputation and influence of the order.

In 1201, a notable event marked the beginning of his term: the king of Armenia seized Fort Gaston, a strategic location in his states and belonging to the Templars. In response, Philippe de Plessiez deployed the Beauséant, the sacred banner of the order, to force the king to return the fort. A truce was agreed upon until the arrival of the legates, reflecting the mutual inability of both parties to achieve a decisive victory. Meanwhile, the king expelled all the Templars from his kingdom and seized their assets. This dispute was not resolved until 1213, to the advantage of the Templars, demonstrating Philippe's perseverance and diplomacy.

The year 1208 brought another major challenge. Pope Innocent III sent a letter to the Templars, reprimanding them for their disobedience towards the bishops and legates. The great wealth accumulated by the order had led to a spirit of unruliness and independence, causing friction with ecclesiastical authority. Despite the papal reprimands, the wealth of the Templars continued to grow, exacerbating tensions with the Church.

In 1210, a glimmer of hope shone on the order when the king of Aragon donated the fort of Azuda and the city of Tortosa to the Templars. This acquisition strengthened their presence in Spain and their ability to resist Muslim incursions.

Three years later, in 1213, the Templars played a decisive role in the famous victory of Ubéda against the Moors of Spain. Among the distinguished knights in this battle, Gomez Ramirez, preceptor of Castile, particularly stood out. His leadership and bravery were noted, although some sources incorrectly designated him as grand master of the order.

The year 1217 was marked by the capture of Alcazar and another significant victory over the Moors. The valour of the Templars, under the leadership of Philippe de Plessiez, was a key element of these military successes. Their ability to conduct sieges and win battles solidified their reputation as formidable warriors and defenders of the Christian faith.

Philippe de Plessiez died in 1217, leaving behind a legacy of strong leadership and resilience in the face of challenges. Under his stewardship, the Templars navigated through internal and external conflicts, strengthening their position in the Holy Land and Europe. His ability to manage crises, negotiate with the powerful of his time, and lead victorious military campaigns made him a respected and memorable grand master.

XIV. William of Chartres (1217-1219).

Guillaume de Chartres, from the illustrious house of the counts of Blois, was the true successor of Philippe de Plessiez to the dignity of Grand Master of the Templars in 1217. He is often wrongly confused with Guillaume de Montredon, but these two characters were distinct, and Montredon never reached the rank of Grand Master.

Under the leadership of Guillaume de Chartres, the Templars undertook ambitious projects to strengthen their strategic positions. Among these projects, the construction of the famous Pilgrims' Castle on the tip of a rock near the sea stood out. This fortress, although very costly to build, proved extremely useful. Its strategic position and robust defences caused more harm to the Muslim forces than many military campaigns. The Pilgrims' Castle became a symbol of the determination and power of the Templars, serving not only as a military bastion but also as a refuge for pilgrims on their way to the holy places.

In 1218, while the Templars were engaged in the siege of Damietta, the Pilgrims' fortress was attacked by enemy forces. However, despite the absence of the knights, the fortress valiantly resisted the assault. This resistance demonstrated the solidity of the defences built under the supervision of Guillaume de Chartres and the effectiveness of the Templars in fortifying and protecting their strategic positions.

The Damietta campaign, in Egypt, was a bold endeavour aimed at weakening Muslim power by controlling a key strategic point. Guillaume de Chartres actively participated in it, demonstrating his commitment to the crusaders' cause. However, the campaign was marked by unexpected difficulties. In 1219, an epidemic caused by the flooding of the Nile devastated the ranks of the crusaders, causing numerous losses.

Guillaume de Chartres succumbed to this epidemic disease in front of the walls of Damietta in 1219. His premature death was a significant loss for the Templars and for all Christian forces in the Holy Land. Despite the brevity of his magisterium, Guillaume left behind a legacy of courage and determination. His leadership during the construction of the Pilgrims' Castle and his active participation in the siege of Damietta testify to his unwavering dedication to the Templar cause.

XV. Pierre de Montaigu (1219-1233).

Pierre de Montaigu, from a family widely spread across France, was named Grand Master of the Templars in 1219, succeeding Guillaume de Chartres in front of Damietta. His bravery and skill demonstrated during this siege earned him flattering comparisons with Gideon, the legendary military leader and judge of Israel.

The siege of Damietta, an integral part of the Fifth Crusade, was a significant event at the beginning of his term. The Christians, determined to bring the war to the heart of the enemy states, besieged this strategic location in 1217. The Templars, under the direction of Montaigu, showed their usual bravery and managed to take the city. However, the reckless intervention of the legate, who interfered in the direction of the enterprise, quickly compromised this triumph. The Christian army, having recklessly advanced into Egypt, found itself in a desperate situation, which forced it to return Damietta and withdraw.

In 1224, the Templars played a decisive role in the campaigns against the Moors in Castile, contributing to great military successes. Their presence in Aragon also proved crucial. In 1225, the order's fortresses served as a refuge for the young king Don Jayme, threatened by the ambitious Moncade who sought to dethrone him.

The year 1227 brought tensions with Emperor Frederick II. In Sicily, Frederick mistreated the Templars for their support of the Pope in his conflicts with him. Despite this dispute, the Templars welcomed Frederick with the honours due to his imperial majesty upon his arrival in the Holy Land in 1228. However, when Frederick demanded their military support, Montaigu refused, citing the papal ban on following the orders of an excommunicated prince. This refusal, as well as Montaigu's refusal to subscribe to the treaty that Frederick had concluded with the Sultan of Egypt in 1229, exacerbated the tensions between them.

The emperor, frustrated and vexed, left Palestine hurling insults at the grand master. Back in Europe, Frederick continued to harass the Templars in Sicily, using his power to vex them.

Despite these conflicts, the Templars continued to expand their influence and conquests. In 1233, the Templars of Aragon, under the orders of King Don Jayme, participated in the conquest of the Balearic Islands. That same year, the king appointed the masters of the Temple and the Hospital as governors for his son and heir, Alfonse, highlighting the trust and importance given to these military orders.

XVI. Armand de Périgord (1233-1234).

Armand de Périgord, from the illustrious house of the counts of Périgord, became Grand Master of the Templars in 1233, succeeding Pierre de Montaigu. Before his election, Armand had served as preceptor of Calabre and Sicily, already demonstrating his leadership skills and commitment to the order.

Armand de Périgord's magisterium was marked by incessant conflicts and considerable challenges. In 1237, he led the Templars to a victory against the Saracens near Aleppo, once again demonstrating the value and military competence of the order. However, this victory was quickly followed by a dramatic setback, from which he only escaped with eight other knights.

At that time, the affairs of Christians in the East were in a deplorable state. The threats were multiple, and the situation became even more complicated with the arrival of the Khwarazmians in 1243. This new race of warriors, unknown until then, swept over Christian lands with unparalleled ferocity. The Khwarazmians, described by historians as men of carnage and blood, sowed destruction wherever they went, bringing death and devastation in their path.

Faced with this threat, the Christians rallied their forces, with the Templars at the forefront. In 1243, the two armies met near Gaza in a horrifying battle that lasted two days. The knights of the military orders, including the Templars, demonstrated extraordinary bravery, performing feats of valour. Despite their courage, they were overwhelmed by the superior numbers of the Khwarazmians. The battle ended in a devastating defeat for the Christians.

The losses were enormous: the Order of the Temple lost 312 knights and 324 arms servants. The bravery of the Templars could not compensate for the numerical inferiority, and almost all the knights fell in battle. Armand de Périgord himself perished heroically at the head of his troops, a tragic end that marked the severity of this defeat.

While waiting for the election of a new grand master, the general chapter appointed Guillaume de Roquefort as vice-manager, tasked with maintaining the direction of the order in these troubled times.

XVII. Guillaume de Sonnac (1247-1250).

The Order of the Templars, though weakened by the terrible losses of the Battle of Gaza, demonstrated extraordinary resilience and determination in recovering from this tragedy. The accounts reported back in Europe painted a poignant picture of the misfortunes of the Holy Land and the heroic bravery of the knights, whose tragic fate seemed unjust given their worth.

However, the glory and courage of the Templars were fertile seeds that soon bore fruit. Quickly, the knights resumed their positions in the sieges and battles, ready to continue their fight for the defence of Christendom.

It is in this troubled context that Saint Louis, determined to rectify the situation of Christians in the Holy Land, undertook his crusade, and Guillaume de Sonnac, from a distinguished family in Rouergue, was elected Grand Master of the Templars in 1247. According to Mathieu-Paris, Guillaume de Sonnac was an old knight, mastering the art of war and renowned for his courage, piety and prudence.

King Saint Louis arrived in Cyprus on September 28, 1248, accompanied by several French Templars. Guillaume de Sonnac joined him in front of Damietta and distinguished himself during the siege of this place, which was finally taken by the crusaders. Saint Louis, continuing his march towards Palestine, ordered the Templars to form the vanguard of his army, with precise instructions given to his brother, Robert, Count of Artois, to follow the Templars with the main body of the army and not to undertake anything without his permission.

In 1250, the crossing of the Nile was accomplished without great difficulties. Robert, with a fervour characteristic of his youth and his desire for glory, pushed back the enemies on the shore, pursued them to their camp, forced the entrenchments and massacred all those who were there. However, the open and abandoned city of Massoure tempted the Count of Artois, and despite the wise advice of Sonnac, he recklessly rushed towards the city at the head of his army. This haste led to a disaster.

While Robert's forces were engaged in looting, the Muslim forces, rallied under the command of Bencdocdar, an officer of great value, launched a devastating counterattack. The Count of Artois and the majority of the knights perished in this massacre, leaving very few survivors. Guillaume de Sonnac, despite the loss of an eye and numerous injuries, managed to return to the camp.

However, three days later, during a new action, Guillaume de Sonnac was killed. His death coincided with the crushing defeat of the crusaders and the capture of King Saint Louis, marking a tragic turning point in this crusade.

XVIII. Renaud de Vichiers (1250-1256).

Renaud de Vichiers, originally from Champagne, became Grand Master of the Templars in 1250, succeeding Guillaume de Sonnac after the knights' return to Palestine. Before his election, Renaud had served as Grand Marshal of the order and Preceptor of France, positions that had allowed him to demonstrate his skills in leadership and military strategy.

Renaud de Vichiers played a crucial role in persuading Saint Louis to extend his stay in Syria. Through his remonstrances, he highlighted the importance of maintaining a Christian presence in the Holy Land, thus convincing the king to continue his efforts to strengthen the positions of the Crusaders.

Shortly after his election, Renaud learned the news of the death of Emperor Frederick II. This news was accompanied by another crucial piece of information: Frederick II's will ordered the restitution of the goods he had confiscated from the Templars. This restitution was a significant victory for the order, strengthening their economic position and their ability to continue their missions.

Under the leadership of Renaud de Vichiers, the Templars continued to play a vital role in the defence of the Latin states of the East. Renaud de Vichiers died in 1256, after six years at the head of the Templars.

XIX. Thomas Béraut or Bérail (1256-1273).

In the year of our Lord 1256, Thomas Béraut was invested with the supreme dignity of Grand Master of the Order of the Templars, succeeding Renaud de Vichiers. Originating from a noble lineage, Béraut inherited a powerful order but continually besieged by Muslim forces and the political intrigues of the time.

Upon his election, Thomas Béraut dedicated himself to strengthening the Templar positions in the Holy Land. Four years after his investiture, in 1260, the Templars of Castile were bravely fighting against the Moors of Andalusia. Meanwhile, in Palestine, the Templar forces were facing a formidable threat: Bondochar, the Sultan of Egypt, defeated them, scattering them or reducing them to prisoners. The defeat inflicted by Bondochar marked a period of great turbulence and increased challenges for the order.

In 1264, Pope Urban IV showed particular hostility towards Étienne de Sissi, marshal of the order, depriving him of his position in an unprecedented decision. Étienne de Sissi protested vigorously, but his response was met with a papal excommunication. The Order of the Templars sided with their marshal, a stance that demonstrated their internal solidarity. Urban IV died shortly after, and Clement IV, his successor, lifted the excommunication after severely reprimanding the superiors of the order. This episode strengthened the cohesion and autonomy of the Templars in the face of papal interference.

The year 1266 brought a new major challenge: Bondochar besieged the fortress of Sephet, under Templar control. The siege was long and difficult. Despite a heroic defence, the defences of Sephet were gradually demolished. The Prior of the Temple, governor of the fortress, had to surrender to the inevitable. The terms of the surrender stipulated that the Christian defenders could withdraw without being disturbed. However, once master of Sephet, Bondochar betrayed this agreement. He offered the captive Christians a few hours to choose between conversion to Islam or death. The Prior of the Temple, assisted by two Franciscans, spent the night urging the defenders and the inhabitants to choose martyrdom. Of the three thousand souls present, only eight renounced their faith. The next day, the survivors were slaughtered, and the Prior, for his courage and firmness, was flayed alive on the sultan's order.

In 1268, Bondochar continued his conquests, wresting the Beaufort castle and several other strongholds located on the borders of Armenia from the Templars. Bondochar's military successes alarmed Christian Europe and were partly responsible for the triggering of a new crusade in 1270. However, despite the numerous reinforcements, the Holy Land quickly found itself without any other support than that of the Templar knights, who continued to desperately defend the last Christian bastions.

During these tumultuous years, the Grand Master Thomas Béraut strived to maintain the cohesion and determination of his knights. His leadership was marked by a wisdom recognized by his contemporaries, as evidenced by a letter from the Easterners to the King of Navarre. Despite his efforts, external and internal challenges weighed heavily on the order.

Bernard the Treasurer reports that Thomas Béraut died on March 25, 1273. His death marked the end of a period of fierce resistance and immense sacrifices for the Templars. However, his magisterium was also tinged with controversies, some claiming that it was under his reign that fatal errors began to spread within the Order of the Temple. These allegations, although they lack concrete evidence, cast a shadow over his legacy, fuelling speculations and accusations that would later emerge against the Templars.

XX. Guillaume de Beaujeu (1273-1294).

Guillaume de Beaujeu, originally from Burgundy and a member of a distinguished family, was elected Grand Master of the Templars on May 13, 1273, according to Bernard the Treasurer. At the time of his election, Guillaume was commander of La Pouille, and his absence during his nomination testifies to the trust and respect he inspired among his peers.

The following year, Guillaume de Beaujeu attended the Council of Lyon, thus demonstrating his commitment to maintaining close ties with the religious and political authorities of the time. On September 28, 1274, he arrived in Palestine, a territory devastated by conflicts. The Templar knights, harassed by Muslim forces, had retreated to the mountains with King Hugues de Lusignan, desperately trying to maintain a defensive position.

In 1276, a particular event marked this period: Don Pédre de Moncade, preceptor of Aragon, was captured by the Moors. Although some wrongly labelled him as the grand master of the Hospitallers, this incident highlighted the vulnerability of Christians in the Holy Land.

Two years later, in 1278, Guillaume de Beaujeu, exasperated by the repeated affronts of Boémond VI, Prince of Antioch, sought revenge. He launched a fleet against the prince, but it perished in a shipwreck, annihilating his hopes of retaliation and illustrating the ever-present risks of military ventures of the time.

The following year, the Templars found themselves in conflict with Alfonse, king of Portugal, who stripped them of numerous assets given by his ancestors. The order brought their complaints to the Pope, who excommunicated the king in response. This dispute, like many others, highlighted the growing tensions between the Templars and the European Christian kingdoms.

In 1283, similar disputes arose with the king of Cyprus, leading to sanctions and papal interventions in an attempt to reconcile the conflicting parties. The papal mediation led to a temporary resolution, but the frictions remained latent, undermining Christian unity in the Holy Land.

The outcome of so many wars and dissensions was tragic. The Christian strongholds in Palestine fell one after the other. By 1289, the Templars only controlled Sidon and the Castle of the Pilgrims. The other

Frankish forces only had Tyre, Acre, and Beirut. Faced with this desperate situation, the king of Cyprus and the knights tried in vain to negotiate peace. They only obtained a two-year truce, quickly broken by adventurers who landed in Acre and treacherously violated the agreement.

In 1291, Sultan Khalil, irritated by these provocations, left Cairo with a powerful army, determined to exterminate the remaining Christians in Syria. Acre, the last significant stronghold of the Crusaders, was attacked by land on April 5, 1291. The siege, conducted with relentless force, put the city under siege. Most of the inhabitants, terrified, abandoned Acre, seeking refuge on departing ships. However, an elite troop mainly composed of Templars and Hospitallers remained to defend the city.

However, on May 18, 1291, Guillaume de Beaujeu was struck under the armpit by a poisoned arrow during a furious assault by Muslim forces. Mortally wounded, he continued to lead the defence with exemplary bravery, but succumbed shortly after, leaving his knights facing a desperate situation.

The fall of Acre marked the end of significant Christian presence in the Holy Land. Guillaume de Beaujeu, through his heroic death, became a symbol of the fierce struggle and determination of the Templars. His bravery and sacrifice were hailed by his contemporaries, and his name has remained etched in memories as that of a great master devoted to the Christian cause until the end.

XXI. Thiébaud Gaudin or Monk Gaudini (1291-1298).

In these times of despair and peril, all eyes turned to Thiébaud Gaudin, also known as Monk Gaudini, recognized as one of the bravest of the Templar order. He succeeded Guillaume de Beaujeu, at a time when the situation was critical. His inauguration took place on a field of carnage, marking a new chapter in the history of the order.

On May 18, 1291, as the assaults of the Muslim forces were at their peak, the city of Acre fell. It was a crushing defeat for the Christian defenders. The few surviving Hospitallers took refuge on the shores of the sea and managed to escape on boats. Among the Templars, about three hundred of them, with the new Grand Master Gaudin, entrenched themselves in the Temple tower, resolved to make their last stand there.

Throughout the following day, they heroically resisted the enemy's relentless assaults. However, the next day, the tower, undermined by the opposing forces, collapsed with a terrifying crash, burying its defenders in its ruins. This tragedy sealed the fate of most of the present Templars.

Of the more than five hundred Templars who had valiantly withstood the siege of Acre, only ten, mutilated and exhausted, managed to escape. Gaudin was one of them. On May 20, he embarked with the treasures of the order and went to Cyprus, accompanied by the Grand Master of the Hospitallers. Together, they established the new headquarters of their orders in the city of Limassol, under the protection of King Henry II. Gaudin, however, did not survive long in this retreat and died by 1298 at the latest.

Thiébaud Gaudin, although his term was short and marked by defeats, symbolized the resilience and indomitable courage of the Templars. His escape from Acre with the order's treasures was an act of preservation in the face of total destruction.

In Cyprus, under the protection of King Henry II, Gaudin attempted to restructure and fortify what remained of the order. However, resources were limited and the challenges immense. Gaudin's death in 1298 marked the end of an era and the beginning of an even darker period for the Templars.

The tragic fate of the Templars in Palestine remains etched in history as a poignant example of bravery, sacrifice, and dedication. The heroic exploits and ultimate sacrifices of these knights continue to inspire and fascinate. Their legacy, despite setbacks, remains a lasting testament to their commitment to defending Christianity.

XXII. Jacques de Molay (1298-1314).

Jacques de Molay first appears in 1298 as the Grand Master of the Templars. Coming from a distinguished family in the county of Burgundy, he was from the land of Molay, located in the deanery of Neublant in the diocese of Besançon. Jacques de Molay had made himself known at the court of France during the baptism of one of the children of King Philip the Fair.

Upon his election, Jacques de Molay found himself immersed in intense conflicts. In 1299, Casan, the king of the Mongol Tartars, came to the aid of the Armenians, and the Templars joined him. Together, they inflicted a defeat on the Muslims and recaptured several places, including Jerusalem, where they remained in garrison. However, this recovery was short-lived. The following year, Jerusalem fell back under Muslim domination, and the fortifications of the Holy City were razed.

In 1301, the grand master, retired on the island of Orade, harassed the Muslim forces to the point of forcing the governor of Phoenicia to ask for reinforcements to repel him. In 1302, an emir came to attack the island, and victory was declared in favour of the Infidels. One hundred and twenty knights were taken prisoner and taken to Cairo, marking a heavy loss for the order.

Despite these setbacks, the Templars continued to fight tooth and nail to reclaim their lands. In 1303, the Templars and the Hospitallers, allied with the troops of Casan, launched new offensives against the Muslims. However, they were severely beaten in two encounters, which forced them to retreat to Cyprus.

In 1306, the Grand Master Jacques de Molay was summoned by the Pope to the court of Avignon. He went there with sixty of his knights, thus demonstrating the persistent power and influence of the order despite the challenges encountered.

The political and religious context in Europe, at that time, was in full turmoil. King Philip the Fair, in particular, harboured ambitions of centralizing power and viewed the influence and wealth of the Templars with disfavour. Their vast possessions, their international network, and their independence constituted a potential threat to his authority.

In 1307, under the influence of Philip the Fair, accusations of heresy, sodomy, and other abominable crimes were brought against the Templars. On Friday, October 13, 1307, a date that will mark history, Philip the Fair ordered the arrest of all the Templars in France. Jacques de Molay, surprised by this sudden attack, was captured along with many other knights.

The accusations against them were based on confessions extorted under torture. The Templars were subjected to brutal interrogations, and many of them confessed to crimes they did not commit. Jacques de Molay himself was tortured, but he stubbornly refused to acknowledge the disgraceful charges brought against the order.

In 1310, a council was convened in Paris to judge the Templars. Jacques de Molay and other high dignitaries of the order were confronted with their accusations. Despite immense pressure, Molay maintained his dignity and loyalty towards his brothers in arms. The order of the Templars was officially dissolved by Pope Clement V in 1312, under pressure from Philip the Fair.

In March 1314, Jacques de Molay and Geoffroy de Charnay, Preceptor of Normandy, were led to the stake in Paris. Refusing to acknowledge the accusations, they proclaimed their innocence and that of the order until their last breath. The scene of their execution was poignant: before a vast crowd, they remained firm and dignified, asserting that the order of the Templars had been unjustly slandered.

According to the chronicles, Jacques de Molay, in his final moments, is said to have cursed Philip the Fair and Pope Clement V, summoning them to appear before the divine tribunal before the end of the year. Strangely, Philip the Fair and Clement V both died within the following year, fuelling legends and myths about the Templars' final moments.

The death of Jacques de Molay marked the end of an era for the Order of the Templars. His courage, dignity, and loyalty in the darkest moments left an indelible impression on history. The Templars, although dissolved, continued to fascinate the collective imagination, becoming symbols of mystery and tragedy.

Today, Jacques de Molay is often perceived as a martyr and a tragic hero. His struggle to defend the honour of the order and his last brave words before perishing on the stake remain etched in history. The legacy of the Templars, although marked by controversy and tragedy, continues to inspire and captivate those who seek to understand the complexities of this tumultuous period.

Thus, the life and death of Jacques de Molay not only illustrate the end of the Templar order, but also the power and corruption of medieval politics, offering a lasting lesson on justice, loyalty, and sacrifice.

Chapter 10: Connections Between the Templars and Pirates.

Beneath the torn veils of time, where the waves of history mingle with the legends of the seas, a fascinating intrigue emerges: the links between the Templars, these sacred knights, and the pirates, these lords of the oceans. Although the paths of the Templars and pirates seem divergent at first glance, a closer examination reveals surprising connections, woven with mystery, hidden treasures, and intertwined destinies.

The Fall of the Templars and the Flight to the Sea.

The abrupt end of the Order of the Templars, marked by the mass arrests of 1307 and the dissolution of the order in 1312, left many knights homeless and without a cause. Hunted by the agents of Philip IV and the inquisitors of the Church, some Templars sought refuge far from European lands. The sea, vast and untamed, offered an ideal escape. Many historians and researchers suggest that fugitive Templars turned to the sea, finding sanctuary among the buccaneers and privateers.

The Templar fleets, powerful and well-equipped, were suddenly without a home port or official mission. Stories and legends tell that these ships mysteriously disappeared, evading royal seizure. Some believe that these ships, with their crews of seasoned knights, became the precursors of pirate fleets, sailing under black flags rather than red crosses.

The Symbols and the Mysteries.

One of the most intriguing links between the Templars and pirates lies in the shared symbols. The Templar's cross pattee, although distinct, is sometimes confused with the pirate's cross. The two symbols, although from different contexts, have become emblematic of rebellion and defiance.

Furthermore, some pirate flags display esoteric and mystical symbols reminiscent of Templar traditions. The famous Jolly Roger, with its skull and crossbones, can be interpreted as a stylized version of the mortuary iconography that the Templars used in their funeral rites. These symbolic similarities fuel theories that pirates may have inherited, in one way or another, the secret traditions of the Templars.

The Hidden Treasures and the Tales of Corsairs.

The tales of hidden treasures are at the heart of legends both of the Templars and pirates. The Templars, before their fall, would have hidden their immense wealth to prevent it from falling into the hands of Philip IV. These treasures, composed of gold, jewels, and sacred relics, would have remained buried, guarded by Templar secrets and mysterious codes.

Pirates, famous for their plundering and buried treasures, are often linked to these legends. Oak Island, in Nova Scotia, is one of the most famous places associated with these hidden treasures. Excavations on the island have revealed artifacts and structures that could be attributed to the Templars, suggesting that the fugitive knights may have buried their treasures in secret locations, protected by ingenious codes and traps.

The Corsairs of Malta and the Templars of Cyprus.

Another possible link between the Templars and pirates is found in the Knights of Malta. After the dissolution of the Templars, the Order of the Hospital of Saint John of Jerusalem, later known as the Knights of Malta, inherited many Templar possessions. These knights, like the Templars, fought against Muslim forces in the Mediterranean, often using corsair tactics.

The Knights of Malta, operating from the island of Malta, became formidable privateers, attacking Muslim ships and using the captured wealth to finance their defences. Some historians suggest that the refugee Templars may have joined the ranks of the Knights of Malta, continuing their struggle under a new banner but with methods similar to those of pirates.

The Brothers of the Coast and the Templar Heritage.

The Brothers of the Coast, a confederation of pirates operating in the Caribbean in the 17th century, are often mentioned in discussions about the links between the Templars and pirates. These pirates, who put up strong resistance to colonial powers, shared a hierarchical structure and a code of conduct that recall Templar traditions.

The Brothers of the Coast advocated for a form of internal democracy, with strict rules for sharing loot and discipline, similar to the rule of the Templars. This structure, although born out of the necessities of piracy, could reflect the influence of wandering knights who had found a new vocation on the seas.

Modern Theories and Legends.

In modern popular culture, the links between the Templars and pirates have been explored through novels, films, and video games. Works like the "Assassin's Creed" series imagine Templars turned pirates, pursuing their quests for treasures and secrets through thrilling high-sea adventures. These narratives, although steeped in fiction, draw on historical and legendary elements to weave captivating stories that continue to fascinate the audience.

Contemporary theories about the Templars and pirates often rely on archaeological clues, historical documents, and popular stories to suggest that the Knights Templar, fleeing after their fall, could have become masters of the seas, using their naval expertise and hidden wealth to finance a new life of freedom and rebellion.

Chapter 11: Templars and Freemasons: Historical Links.

Beneath the arcana of history, shrouded in mystery and enigma, the figures of the Templars and Freemasons stand, surrounded by legends and speculations. Although separated by centuries, these two fraternities are often associated in the collective imagination, their destinies intertwined by tales of secrecy, power, and concealed knowledge.

The Origins of the Templars and Freemasons.

The Templars, founded in the early 12th century, were monk-soldiers dedicated to the protection of pilgrims in the Holy Land and the defence of the Crusader states. Their order, recognized for its military discipline and religious devotion, quickly prospered, accumulating wealth and influence until their abrupt dissolution in 1312.

The Freemasons, whose precise origins remain partly obscure, later emerged in the 17th century as a fraternity of builders and thinkers. Speculative masonry, developed from the medieval guilds of stonecutters, became a philosophical and esoteric organization, attracting members from various backgrounds, united by ideals of fraternity, freedom, and the pursuit of truth.

The Legend of the Templar Continuity.

One of the most persistent legends linking the Templars and the Freemasons is that of the Templar continuity. According to this theory, the Templars, after their dissolution, would have found refuge among the builder guilds in Scotland and elsewhere, bringing with them their secrets and traditions. These guilds, by absorbing the Templars, would have evolved to become modern Freemasonry.

Supporters of this theory point to certain Masonic rituals and symbols reminiscent of those of the Templars. For example, the Maltese cross, crossed swords, and Latin mottos are elements shared by both fraternities. These similarities fuel the idea that the Templars may have passed on their esoteric knowledge and initiatory practices to the early Masonic lodges.

The Communal Symbols and Rituals.

Symbols play a central role in both orders, serving as means of communication and spiritual reflection. The Templars used crosses, swords, and architectural motifs in their coats of arms and buildings, symbolizing their sacred mission and their quest for spiritual perfection.

The Freemasons, for their part, use masonry tools - such as the compass, the square and the level - in their rituals, symbolizing the principles of moral and spiritual architecture. These tools, although practical in appearance, are imbued with deep meanings, representing the construction of the individual and the ideal society.

Another shared element is the use of complex initiation ceremonies, aimed at transforming the individual and fully integrating them into the fraternity. Templar and Masonic initiation ceremonies, although different in their specific content, share a symbolic structure and a common goal: that of guiding the initiate towards a deeper understanding of oneself and the universe.

The Manuscripts and The Archives.

Historical documents and manuscripts have been cited as potential evidence of links between the Templars and the Freemasons. One of the most famous documents is the "Larmenius Charter", allegedly drafted in 1324, which describes the transmission of Templar authority to a new lineage of leaders, thus perpetuating the order in secret. Although the authenticity of this document is disputed, it fuels speculation about the clandestine survival of the Templars.

Other documents, such as the Anderson's Constitutions of 1723, which govern speculative Freemasonry, allude to an ancient tradition of builders and esoteric knowledge passed down through the ages. These texts, although not explicitly mentioning the Templars, evoke a lineage of knowledge and practices that could include Templar influence.

The Kadosh Knights and The Scottish Rites.

A particularly interesting link is found in the Ancient and Accepted Scottish Rite of Freemasonry, where there are degrees called "Knight Kadosh" or "Knight Templar". These degrees, among the highest in the rite, are imbued with chivalric symbolism and references to the persecution of the Templars.

The rituals of the Knight Kadosh include symbolic vengeance ceremonies against Philip IV and Pope Clement V, the individuals responsible for the fall of the Templars. These rituals aim to honour the memory of the martyr knights and to convey a message of justice and loyalty to higher ideals. The presence of these degrees in Freemasonry reinforces the idea of a spiritual and symbolic continuity with the order of the Templars.

Contemporary Theories and Criticisms.

Despite the many points of convergence, theories linking the Templars to the Freemasons are not without criticism. Many historians highlight the absence of concrete and direct evidence of a historical continuity between the two orders. They argue that the symbolic and ritual similarities could result from the common influence of Gnostic and esoteric traditions, rather than a direct transmission from the Templar order.

The Freemasons themselves are divided on this issue. Some enthusiastically embrace the idea of a Templar lineage, seeing in these stories a source of prestige and historical depth. Others, more sceptical, prefer to emphasize the autonomy and unique evolution of Freemasonry, without resorting to controversial historical affiliations.

The Role of Legends and the Imaginary.

The legends and stories surrounding the Templars and Freemasons play a crucial role in their appeal and mystique. The figure of the Templar, a devoted and martyred knight, and that of the Freemason, a seeker of truth and builder of light, embody universal ideals of courage, spiritual quest, and fraternity.

These stories, even when they are more fictional than historical, feed the collective imagination and enrich the symbolic tradition of each order. The novels, films and works of art that explore these themes contribute to perpetuating the aura of mystery and fascination that surrounds the Templars and the Freemasons.

Chapter 12: Lessons Learned from the History of the Templars.

Beneath the veils woven with mysteries and legends, the history of the Templars remains a powerful and edifying narrative, rich in lessons for humanity. From the heights of their glory to the depth of their fall, the Templars embody a living parable of bravery, dedication, power, and betrayal. By scrutinizing the annals of their existence, we can extract valuable lessons that still resonate today.

The Strength of Devotion and Faith.

The Templars were above all men of faith. Their commitment to the defence of pilgrims and holy places, despite the dangers and challenges, illustrates the transformative power of devotion. This unwavering dedication, rooted in a deep belief in a cause greater than themselves, drove them to perform acts of extraordinary courage and sacrifice.

This lesson of faith and devotion transcends the centuries. It reminds us that commitment to a noble cause can give meaning to life and inspire heroic actions. Faith, whether religious or philosophical, can be a powerful driving force, capable of overcoming the most arduous trials and achieving seemingly unattainable goals.

Discipline and Organization.

The Templars were renowned for their rigorous discipline and exemplary military organization. Their success on the battlefields and their lasting influence largely stemmed from their strict hierarchical structure and strict code of conduct. This discipline, which encompassed all aspects of their life, allowed them to maintain remarkable unity and efficiency, even in the face of considerable adversity.

From this rigor, we learn the importance of discipline and organization in achieving collective goals. In our modern enterprises, whether they are personal, professional or community-based, the application of disciplined principles and clear organization can transform visions into tangible realities. The Templars teach us that strength lies not only in individual bravery, but also in structured cohesion and cooperation.

Power and its Dangers.

The meteoric rise of the Templars, amassing wealth and influence, offers a mirror on the inherent dangers of power. Their wealth, derived from donations and their role as bankers for European kingdoms, attracted envy and suspicion. This concentration of power and resources eventually led to their downfall, initiated by a king eager to seize their riches and neutralize an influence he perceived as a threat.

Their history illustrates a crucial lesson about power: it is double-edged. The accumulation of wealth and influence can incite envy and fear, leading to betrayals and conflicts. For those who hold power, this lesson is a constant reminder of the need for prudence, transparency, and integrity. Power, without a solid ethical foundation and prudent management, can become a source of vulnerability rather than strength.

The Importance of Justice and Truth

The trials of the Templars, marked by confessions obtained under torture and unfounded accusations, are a dark chapter in judicial history. They remind us of the dangers of justice corrupted by political and personal interests. The manipulation of truth and the abuse of power to achieve hidden objectives led to one of the most notorious injustices of medieval history.

From this episode, we draw an essential lesson about the importance of justice and truth. A society that allows corruption and manipulation to thrive in its judicial institutions condemns itself to repeat the mistakes of the past. The quest for justice must be guided by a sincere search for truth, protected from external influences and personal ambitions.

Resilience and the Pursuit of Truth

Despite their fall, the Templars left a lasting legacy. Their resilience in the face of persecution and their ability to inspire legends and spiritual and philosophical movements testify to their profound influence. The Templars teach us the value of resilience, the ability to rise and persist despite adversity.

This resilience is a valuable lesson for our time. Faced with challenges and setbacks, the ability to persevere and maintain one's convictions is essential. The fall of the Templars reminds us that even in the darkest moments, the human spirit can find ways to survive and leave a lasting legacy.

The Quest for Knowledge and Mystery

Finally, the history of the Templars is steeped in mysteries and legends, from hidden treasures to esoteric knowledge. Their quest for truth and commitment to higher ideals have inspired generations of seekers and mystics. The Templars embody the incessant quest for knowledge, the desire to understand the mysteries of the universe, and to transcend the limits of the known.

This quest for knowledge is a universal lesson. It encourages us to remain curious, to explore the boundaries of our understanding, and to seek deeper truths. In a constantly evolving world, the thirst for knowledge and the willingness to explore the unknown are powerful drivers of progress and personal fulfilment.

Conclusion: An Eternal Legacy

The Templars, through their glorious and tragic history, leave us a legacy rich in lessons. Their devotion, discipline, management of power, struggle for justice, resilience, and quest for knowledge are themes that still resonate today. They remind us that the fundamental values of courage, truth, and perseverance transcend time and eras.

Reflecting on the history of the Templars invites us to apply these lessons in our contemporary lives. Their legacy inspires us to live with integrity, seek justice, persevere in the face of adversity, and relentlessly pursue the quest for truth and knowledge. The Templars, through their history, continue to teach and guide us, their light traversing the centuries to illuminate our path.

Dear Reader,

What did you think?

I hope you enjoyed this adventure as much as I enjoyed writing it. If you liked this book, I would greatly appreciate it if you could leave your thoughts in a review on Amazon. Just scan the QR code below:

I would also be delighted to receive your comments directly. Feel free to contact me via email at the following address: **contact@claudiobocchia.ch**

Your feedback and suggestions are valuable to me; they help me constantly improve and spread the word about this book to more readers.

Thank you again for your support and see you soon for new adventures!

Best regards, Claudio Bocchia

P.S.: Latest releases, events, bonuses, and more. Receive all my updates by subscribing to the newsletter: **https://claudiobocchia.ch/newsletter**

Find more books from the same publisher Sigma Thotmes Publishing by scanning the QR code:

Printed in Great Britain
by Amazon